P9-BBO-349

DWARF

Courtesy of author

TIFFANIE DIDONATO graduated from the University of Massa-chusetts at Dartmouth with a BFA in writing and communi-cations. She's now a weekly columnist for the magazine *Encore* (encorepub.com) and is stationed with her husband at Camp Lejeune in North Carolina. Visit facebook.com/dwarfmemoir.

Brenna Britton

RENNIE DYBALL is an editor at People.com and a longtime writer for *People* magazine. She has coauthored two books, Christian Siriano's *Fierce Style*, and *A Famous Dog's Life* with Hollywood animal trainer Sue Chipperton. Rennie is a proud Penn State University graduate and lives with her husband in New York City. Visit renniedyball.com.

# DWARF

## A MEMOIR

## Tiffanie DiDonato
### with Rennie Dyball

A PLUME BOOK

PLUME
Published by the Penguin Group
Penguin Group (USA) Inc., 375 Hudson Street, New York, New York 10014, U.S.A. • Penguin
Group (Canada), 90 Eglinton Avenue East, Suite 700, Toronto, Ontario, Canada M4P 2Y3 (a divi-
sion of Pearson Penguin Canada Inc.) • Penguin Books Ltd., 80 Strand, London WC2R 0RL,
England • Penguin Ireland, 25 St. Stephen's Green, Dublin 2, Ireland (a division of Penguin
Books Ltd.) • Penguin Group (Australia), 250 Camberwell Road, Camberwell, Victoria 3124,
Australia (a division of Pearson Australia Group Pty. Ltd.) • Penguin Books India Pvt. Ltd., 11
Community Centre, Panchsheel Park, New Delhi – 110 017, India • Penguin Group (NZ), 67
Apollo Drive, Rosedale, Auckland 0632, New Zealand (a division of Pearson New Zealand Ltd.)
• Penguin Books (South Africa) (Pty.) Ltd., 24 Sturdee Avenue, Rosebank, Johannesburg 2196,
South Africa

Penguin Books Ltd., Registered Offices: 80 Strand, London WC2R 0RL, England

First published by Plume, a member of Penguin Group (USA) Inc.

First Printing, December 2012
10 9 8 7 6 5 4 3 2 1

Ⓟ REGISTERED TRADEMARK—MARCA REGISTRADA

LIBRARY OF CONGRESS CATALOGING-IN-PUBLICATION DATA
DiDonato, Tiffanie.
  Dwarf : a memoir / Tiffanie DiDonato with Rennie Dyball.
    p. cm.
  ISBN 978-0-452-29811-8
  1. DiDonato, Tiffanie—Health. 2. Diastrophic dwarfism. 3. Bone lengthening (Orthopedics)
4. Dwarfs—Biography.   I. Dyball, Rennie. II. Title.
  RJ135.D53 2012
  599.9'49—dc23
  [B]          2012009982

Printed in the United States of America
Set in Goudy Old Style Std
Designed by Eve L. Kirch

PUBLISHER'S NOTE
This is a work of nonfiction. Some names and identifying details have been altered in order to
protect the privacy of particular individuals. Everything herein is based on the author's own memories and recollections.

Penguin is committed to publishing works of quality and integrity.
In that spirit, we are proud to offer this book to our readers;
however, the story, the experiences, and the words
are the author's alone.

To my mom, the strongest woman I know.
I will never stop fighting.

# CONTENTS

# ACKNOWLEDGMENTS

DAD, THANK YOU for always viewing me as your little pumpkin pie. See, it's all worth it. I love you. "Please, sir or madam, will you read my book? It took me years to write, will you take a look?"

Papa, thank you for your warm embrace, comforting smile, and tears of joy and happiness that morning by your pool. I am grateful to be a DiDonato.

Dr. Mortimer, I hope you know that I always viewed you as more than simply my doctor. You are a part of my family. I don't have enough space within this book to adequately thank you for all you have done for me throughout the years. Among the gifts of love, trust, understanding, and compassion, you have also given me a chance to be free. I hope I didn't let you down.

Dr. Shapiro, wherever you are, I have not, nor will I ever, forget you. I hope when this book debuts our paths get the chance to meet again.

To the UMass nurses, thank you for the support to my mom not just during the entire bone-lengthening procedure, but throughout my entire life. You all are too unrecognized for the compassion you give to patients and to one another. You deserve more. I love you.

Marlborough High School, though I left you and assumed you forgot me, my heart is elated to learn you have always considered and thought of me. For the first time, I can say I truly have Panther Pride.

Rennie, over the course of working together you have become so much more than my coauthor. You have become my friend, my sister, my coach—my family. With your guidance, I've grown a little bit more in this crazy world of ours. Thank you for the great big bowls of laughter and tough love throughout it all.

Mollie, there are absolutely no words to describe how thankful I am for your undying belief and dedication. I've come across so many who have doubted my capability, but you helped me prove them all wrong. You have my trust, my loyalty, and my love, always. Thank you.

Becky, thank you for not just listening to my story, but for hearing it inside your heart. Just when I think I've gained all the inches I can, you give me a platform to stand on. I feel taller than ever.

Shea Carver, you taught me to "relax and have a cocktail." You gave me my first chance to be heard beyond the face of my PC. I'm honored to call you my friend.

Ken Rotcop, because of your persistence, guidance and love, *this* is a reality.

Phi Sigma Sigma, Theta Sigma Chapter, you are all responsible for some of the greatest moments of my life. And though I can't jot them all down, know that without you all my growth as a woman and a sister would have surely been stunted—LITP Ladies!

Importantly, to my husband, because of you I live a *real* fairy tale. You are my hero, my knight, and my everything. I'd walk through hell just to hold your hand. Always and forever, I love you.

Last, but not least, a close family friend of mine once said, "There is no greater return than to thank the one person who hurt you most, for making you a tougher person." Ms. Hart, thank you.

RENNIE DYBALL would like to thank Tiffanie for the privilege of helping you tell your story. You've inspired me to appreciate life in a whole new way.

To our wonderful editor, Becky Cole, thank you for such a fun, rewarding collaboration, and to the team at Plume for all your hard work.

Thanks to my agent, Mollie Glick, for your endless help, wisdom, and humor each step of the way. Here's to working on many more books together.

Mom, you're the best uncredited editor anyone could ever hope for. Thanks for always listening, reading, and believing in me. John, thank you for supporting me in everything I do—I couldn't ask for a better champion in my corner. And to my dad: for the killer instinct, for seeing a writer in your crazy little girl all those years ago, and so much more.

# PROLOGUE

# Call Me Tiffanie

On vacation at York Beach in Maine, age six.

BELIEVE IT OR not, I actually enjoyed watching *Snow White and the Seven Dwarfs* as a child. We never owned the video, but it wasn't because my average-size parents wanted to protect their child with dwarfism. I just happened to love *Winnie the Pooh* more, so *Snow White* was just a renter.

I bring this up because it's a question I'm often asked. For the record, I never equated myself with Happy, Dopey, Sleepy, or Sneezy. I did get grumpy growing up, but I promise you there was no correlation.

Another question I get asked a lot is: "Do you see yourself as a dwarf?"

The answer is no.

I do not consider myself a dwarf and I never have. The truth is, it never even occurred to me to do so until people used it to define me in high school, and then later insisted I *wasn't* a dwarf because I'd changed my body and become taller, but I'll get to that.

I don't like the term "dwarf," but I do love confronting it and manipulating it to my advantage. It's a very powerful word and I'll never run from it. That's why I put it on the cover of this book. This is my chance to define the word on my own terms.

While we're on the topic, I don't like the word "midget," either. Not because of the meaning of the word, but because of the way it's used. The word itself is jagged, meant to prick. "Midget" is often used as a label or, like the word "fuck" or "shit," to hurt rather than explain.

So let's be perfectly clear:

I am not a Midget.

I am not a Dwarf.

Please, just call me Tiffanie.

I have a condition called diastrophic dysplasia. I'll save you the trip to Wikipedia: it's a very rare type of dwarfism that results in short stature, joint deformities, and very short arms and legs. From birth to age twelve, my arms were so short that I couldn't reach my own ears, or other parts of my body for that matter.

As a child, I stood three feet, eight inches tall, and I wasn't expected to grow any more. Today, I am four foot ten, thanks to a set of radical bone-lengthening surgeries I underwent to gain independence. Most people gain just two or three inches from the procedure, but I had bigger plans. It's not like I had plastic surgery because I didn't like the way my face looked. Undergoing bone-lengthening surgery was about becoming independent and being able to get from point A to point B in a timely manner, perhaps while carrying some belongings with me at the same time. The body I was born with wouldn't allow me that simple exercise in freedom.

For years, I was consumed by visions of what my life could be like after bone-lengthening surgery. I wanted to drive a car without extensions bolted to the pedals. I wanted to shop for clothes that fit my age, not just my body. I wanted to do the everyday tasks that my family and friends did effortlessly, unknowingly taking their abilities for granted. I desperately wanted to take out the trash. Of all things! I fantasized about picking up the burgeoning white bag with the tie top and walking it out to the garage. I dreamed of reaching the fourth shelf in my refrigerator, the faucet, the light switch, and the coffeemaker. I wanted independence, freedom from the tools and devices I depended on for a normal life. And I didn't think twice about sacrificing to get it.

When most people think of a dwarf, they might picture those with dwarfism who appear on TV. Many of those individuals, such as Amy and Zach from *Little People, Big World*, have a condition called achondroplasia. It's among the most common types of dwarfism (there are actually hundreds of types) but it's a different condition from the one I have—variations on a theme, really.

That's the technical part of it. But the word "dwarf" evokes many other images. I'm not a small, stocky, imaginary being who resembles a human. I don't like to climb mountains, and I don't mine or hunt for buried treasure. I am not fictional, or malevolent, nor do I carry an ax or have magic powers. However, there are a few people I'd like to make disappear.

When I look at myself in the mirror, I see my brown eyes, my thick brown hair, the curve of my mouth, and the crinkle of my nose. If I were to think of myself as merely a dwarf, it would minimize the person I am. And that person is more than a little tired of all these terms people use to define me.

According to the Little People of America (LPA), a dwarf is someone who stands four feet, ten inches or smaller. I happen to be exactly that height. So does that make me a dwarf? Am I still considered a dwarf if I wear my two-inch heels? What about when I take my shoes off and go barefoot? It's like I'm morphing—now I'm a dwarf. Wait, now I'm not!

Dwarf is just a word.

I, on the other hand, am a woman with ideas, talent, and a sharp tongue. I'm a fighter, a military wife, and an opinionated writer. I'm passionate and ridiculously stubborn, and I have a hot Italian temper. I'm fiery, strong willed, and compassionate. I love to love others, and I love to be loved in return.

In October 2008, when *Good Morning America* did a story about my limb-lengthening surgeries, the show's bulletin board blew up with commentary from perfect strangers. I noticed someone from the LPA awarded me the title of E.L.P., or Extended Little Person. I could barely wrap my mind around that one. Why is it so important to slap a label on me? The whole thing gave me such a headache that I needed some E.R.H.M. (extended relief headache medicine).

The acronym implied, yet again, that I needed to be categorized, which is ironic, considering that the purpose of the LPA is to declassify, create equal access, promote integration, and educate. After my TV segment aired, I received hate mail from little people and average-size people alike. All of them criticized me for changing my body.

I just wanted to be able to reach the sink in a public restroom. I wanted to drive a car. I wanted to take care of myself and to do the small, everyday tasks that most people take for granted. Was that too much to ask?

I realize that by putting my story out for everyone, I have the chance to demystify what it's like to be a dwarf. But the truth is, there isn't an invitation-only society or secret handshake. I also understand that, as human beings, we will inherently ask questions about our differences. Some feel the need to classify or label things they don't understand. I'm not starting a one-woman crusade to stop that.

Instead, I want to inspire. I've been through a lot, and I know that others are facing hardships, too. I'm living proof that the seemingly impossible can be overcome.

It's okay with me if you picked up this book because you're curious about what it's like to live with dwarfism. But I hope that you'll take away much more—about freedom, finding independence, and adapting to the world when it won't adapt to you.

As of the writing of this memoir, I am thirty-one years old, and I am blessed with more happiness than I could have ever wished for. I am married to my dream man and living life on my terms with the independence I fought so hard to gain.

Yes, technically, I am a dwarf. But while it might be the title of my book, it does not define me, nor does it precede my name.

My name is Tiffanie. And this is my story.

# DWARF

◆

# CHAPTER 1

# Third-Degree Dwarfism

At age two with my father at
a local amusement park.

MOST PEOPLE DESCRIBE their earliest memory as merely a hazy recollection, like a scene from a dream that blurs around the edges with time. Mine is no different, with one minor exception—something that I remember with all the detail and clarity as if they were right in front of me, right now.

The plaster casts on my legs.

When I was two years old, I underwent one of the first of many surgeries to correct my ill-formed bones. My rare form of dwarfism, diastrophic dysplasia, caused my bones and joints to develop irregularly, so surgical procedures were a part of my life from the start. This procedure was to straighten my clubbed feet, making them more functional and enabling me to walk like other toddlers. I'd had casts on my feet before, beginning when I was three days old. I don't remember the surgery or the recovery, or any pain involved, really. But I do remember those casts.

In this recollection, I'm in my crib, holding my legs as high as I can above my *Sesame Street* blanket and staring at the thick white shells engulfing both of my feet. I'm amazed that no matter how hard I hit them, they won't crack like an egg. They are heavy, cakelike, and smell like plaster and dust.

My little room is decorated with plastic jungle animal decals stuck to each of the walls. There are lions, rhinos, giraffes, and birds, all dancing around me. But I am the one stuck in a cage. Across my room, the door is partially closed, which is upsetting to me because I can't see out into the hallway. I have to see. I have to be out *there*. Raising my legs as high as they will go, I smash them down again against the bars of my pen. Nothing happens. I'm still stuck.

I can also recall sitting down for meals in my Winnie the Pooh high chair, probably because of the song that my mom sang to me each time I was in there. It was a silly little tune, but it was a mealtime staple, just like putting on my bib or clicking into place the little plastic tray on my chair.

*You may be little, you may be short, but I love you, because you're mine,* Mom always sang.

I was five pounds, four ounces when I made my easy entrance into the world on November 12, 1980. "You were two poops and a push," Mom says of my birth. I've never asked her to elaborate because it sounds really gross, but I'm assuming she means she had an easy delivery and wasn't in labor for that long. Time and time again, my mother has told me that my arrival was the happiest moment of her life. *I* was the happiest moment of her life. Even as a small child, I understood that to be true.

As my mom held me and squeezed my tiny wrinkly hands, my dad left the room and called everyone he knew.

"You curled your legs up and settled into a little ball on my chest," Mom tells me. It was such a joyful time that no one noticed that anything was wrong. Yet.

Once the doctors recorded my stats and gave me a more thorough examination, they noticed my arms were shorter than normal. Then they realized my legs were unusually short as well. That's when you could say the two poops hit the fan.

As my mom watched my dad perch proudly on the windowsill after making his rounds on the phone, the on-call pediatrician came into the room.

"Your daughter has third-degree dwarfism," she said.

Then, as quickly as the doctor had entered the room, she turned and exited, leaving panic in her wake.

"If your father could have fallen out of that window he would have, but lucky for him, it was closed," Mom says every time she reflects on that day.

My parents were silent, contemplating many questions that neither one of them could answer. What was dwarfism? How severe was third-degree dwarfism? Was that like third-degree burns? Would the condition get worse?

No one knew.

No further explanation was provided.

The next day, the doctor's confusing diagnosis still loomed over my dad, intensifying his new fears about having a disabled child. He relayed the news to his parents. In a conversation filled with fear, ignorance, and panic, a suggestion was made behind closed doors.

Give the baby up for adoption or get a divorce.

Turns out, there is actually no such thing as "third-degree dwarfism." That was just a generic way to refer to the fact that I was born with a disorder that caused short stature and unusual bone structure. The diagnosis of diastrophic dysplasia would come much later.

But the damage was done.

And with the two options presented to her from my dad's conversation, Mom made *her* decision without a moment's hesitation. Divorce.

Over the course of about six months, she moved us out of my dad's apartment in Webster, Massachusetts, and into a place of our own. Together, just the two of us, Mom and I settled into the tiny, two-bedroom apartment she'd rented in a Cape-style house. She describes it as bright, sunny, and painted yellow—despite the sadness of the divorce, it was a happy little home. Mom made sure that it was. At the time, she was working for a big computer company in the same town. She went to the office from seven a.m. to three p.m. while I went to KinderCare. At dinnertime each night, she sang me her little tune.

*You may be little, you may be short, but I love you, because you're mine!*

Such was our life early on. My mother didn't think about being a single parent to a child with dwarfism; it was just Mom and Tiffie. But before long, the phone calls began.

Dad called her over and over, describing the nightmares of a life without us that haunted him. He said that he saw my eyes every time he went to sleep. Life without his little girl was too much to bear. This story always reminds me of Scrooge and the three ghosts—I picture my dad alone in bed, being visited by the ghosts of his Past, Present, and Future.

First, I imagine him traveling back in time to the night he met my mom at the Driftwood, a popular club in Northborough, Massachusetts, in the '70s. Mom went to the Driftwood with her friend Debbie every Friday night when she got off work. In the beginning, she didn't even like my dad. She thought he was rude and annoying. But as the Friday nights went by, she warmed up to his odd sense of humor and his classic '70s mustache. Before long, they were riding his Harley up Mount Wachusett together and planning their future.

Next, I picture my father dropped back into the sadness of the present situation shortly after my birth. He's all alone and left to think about life without the family he helped create. Finally, I see the third ghost hovering over him with images of the future cutting through the darkness of his lonely apartment.

Dad needed us back in his life, he told Mom, and he asked her for the most difficult gift anyone can give: forgiveness. For that, I've always thought of him as the bravest man I know. In turn, Mom found her own hidden virtue, and she forgave him. But she would never forget.

I may have been little. I may have been short. But I was loved, because I was theirs.

When the April showers of 1981 had passed, May's flowers sprang up all around a little three-bedroom ranch in Douglas, Massachusetts. It was short on curb appeal, but the property held just enough beauty to pique my mom's interest. The house had a happy, bright feel, and it was painted yellow like the color she loved so much in our old apartment. It had no porch—just three drab concrete steps to the front door—and a steep driveway, but to Mom it had all the makings of our first real home.

We moved in right away, even though there was no refrigerator, washing machine, stove, or dryer in the new house. Mom had only a tiny cooler for my milk and juice and a countertop toaster oven where she prepared meals. My parents' relationship gradually fell back into place, as did the necessities. Dad was still living in Webster at the time, but he saved every quarter, dime, nickel, and penny in his Folgers coffee cans until he had enough to buy my mom her first refrigerator. The washer, dryer, and stove came later, along with the jungle animal decals that decorated the walls of my room. Everything my dad did back in those days was penance for what had happened shortly after I was born.

As the weeks went by, Dad remained devoted to taking care of me and to making our lives easier. And that did more than just ease the incredible guilt he lived with (and still does today)—it allowed Mom to pursue her dream of becoming a nurse. Shortly after reconciling with my dad, Mom enrolled in nursing school at the hospital where it all began.

• ◆ •

I had been far too young to remember my parents' nearly failed marriage, and while I was aware that I never saw one of my grandmothers, my parents never made a big deal out of it. But when I was five, something shifted, and gifts began arriving at my house.

At first I didn't realize they were for me. I thought they kept coming to the wrong house, since they always got sent back. But, oh, was I jealous of the kid who got to keep them!

Every week there was something new. I'd wake up in the morning and shuffle out of my bedroom, peeking around the corner to see what new doll, stuffed animal, or toy had arrived. I walked with an unusual gait as a child, just as I had as a toddler, and was a lot slower than other kids my age. I noticed this, but my parents never said anything about it to me, so I didn't regard it as a problem.

Just as quickly as the gifts arrived, my mom would insist that my dad take them away. I always wondered where he was going with them. Was there a secret store? Was he bringing the toys to someone else's house? I wanted to go, too. I always hoped I'd be allowed to get in the car with my dad and see the home of this very lucky little girl.

Mom tried to shield me from the presents. But I often saw them before they were sent away. And even though I didn't actually get to play with the stuffed animals and toys, I loved them just the same.

One day, I noticed that two Cabbage Patch dolls had arrived in the dining room. They were twin boys, and the sight of them in their yellow overalls with their curly, yarn-loop hair was almost too much for me to bear. As I pined over the dolls, taking in their sweet features from a safe distance, my parents were locked in an argument in the kitchen. Dad was pleading with Mom to let me keep the gifts.

"She's trying to show she's sorry! She's admitting she was wrong," Dad said. "I don't understand. Why won't you won't let Tiffie have the gifts?"

"I cannot be bought," my mother responded in a growl. It scared me to hear her use that voice. It reminded me of a monster. "Your *daughter* cannot be bought!"

Mom demanded that Dad send back this latest round of gifts, just as she always did. But this time, I couldn't allow him to do it. I loved them too much. The Cabbage Patch twins were different from the other presents—they were wearing overalls, just like I did, and they had bibs with tiny pockets. I pictured myself taking care of the twins and, when they were good, buying them tiny trinkets from the toy store, like my dad did for me, and tucking the treasures inside those small pockets for safekeeping. I simply *had* to have those dolls.

So I dashed out from the doorway and headed straight toward the twins, screaming with happiness.

"They're for *me!*" I cried out. "Please don't take them! Please!" No one said anything.

Wildly, I looked from one parent to the other. "Who are they from?" I asked.

My mom looked like she'd been slapped in the face.

"Do you understand why now, Gerry?"

My dad nodded. Finally, he answered me. "They're from me, pumpkin pie," he lied.

These were the last gifts ever to arrive. And the only ones I was allowed to keep from my grandmother Pauline.

CHAPTER 2

# Move Over, MacGyver

Striking a pose at my
aunt Jean's pool, age six.

I SPENT A SIGNIFICANT PART of my childhood molding myself into
the epitome of self-sufficiency: I turned into a mini MacGyver. At
age five, I trained my eye to spot random household items that
could serve beyond their original, singular functions to help me
live my life. I would have made MacGyver proud, too, since the
tools I used were no more complicated than a pair of salad tongs.

For a while, I hardly knew there was a difference between me
and the other children. None of my friends could reach the bathroom sink or successfully navigate their way through heavy doors,
so there was nothing outstanding about me there. But as my
friends got older, they also grew taller and started reaching things
I couldn't, like light switches and door handles.

Still, I never felt disabled. I never felt held back by my body, merely challenged. Every obstacle became a game, and I always wanted to win. With each daily challenge my mind expanded. Though my stature didn't change, I grew more creative. Maneuvering through my days, I manipulated chairs into ladders and used them to reach clothes in my closet, to see out the window, and to reach the dials on my dad's stereo system and the Disney videos on the middle shelf of the entertainment center.

The most important piece of weaponry in my early battles with dwarfism was a pair of seriously versatile salad tongs. With them, I could reach, grab, and squeeze. I could push off my socks and tug my underwear away from my ankles and up my thighs. I could hook and pull just about anything. I could also do what many would never consider to be a problem. With tongs, I could accomplish what average-size people understandably take for granted.

I could grip toilet paper and wipe myself.

I had no idea what others struggled with in the bathroom, and no one in my family pointed out that using tongs to wipe was something out of the ordinary. I simply did as many others with dwarfism must do. Since my short arms would not allow me to reach my private areas with my hand, I adapted. I could wait for someone to clean me (as my mom did for the first several years of my life), find a creative way to do it myself, or worst of all, skip wiping entirely. The choice was a no-brainer.

We all do things that we aren't proud of in war.

An average pencil served as my lance to hit various light switches around my home. Turning them off, however, was more difficult and required a separate device. A spatula worked fine. If that wasn't available, I just left them on.

A towel, if my dad was lazy enough to leave one on the bathroom floor, served as a net. With a swing or a slap, I could trap just about anything and drag it toward me.

My mom's cookbooks rarely stayed on the lower bookshelf in the living room where she housed them. Instead, I stacked them in front of the sink so I could wash my hands. Each *How to Cook* hardcover, *Chicken Made Simple* bible, and Julia Child masterpiece could be pushed across the tile floor with ease. They piled nicely against the bottom kitchen cabinets, forming makeshift stairs.

Countertops became platforms on which I stood to reach bowls, cups, and plates. My favorite one, a white porcelain soup bowl with an oversized flattened handle, was always stacked on the second shelf in the upper cabinet. Like an acrobat, I perfected the art of balancing and bending and, with careful manipulation, I could grab that soup bowl like any other. I felt like a treasure hunter.

"Jesus Christ!" my mom once screamed when she found me atop the counter during the hunt. "You'll break your neck! What are you doing?"

"I want cereal," I replied simply.

"Why didn't you ask me to get it?"

"Because I can do it," I said, almost offended that she felt the need to ask. She knew me better than that.

It was during times like these that she was thinking about her father, my "Papa," who had very strong beliefs about the way I should be raised.

Papa—Robert Pryor—always reminded me of Popeye the Sailor, but with ice blue eyes like his favorite singer, Frank Sinatra. Papa did not have a single tattoo, nor did he smoke from a pipe, but he was a navy Seabee who was strong, full of pride, and honest (sometimes too honest)—when he spoke, his voice commanded the room. My mom followed in his footsteps. Other people's opinions simply didn't matter to my mom and Papa.

Whenever he would visit, Papa always told my mother how important it was for me to do things myself. He wanted me to be independent and to be treated like any other kid. This, he believed, was the key for me to live my life to the fullest. Inspirational articles about overcoming adversity arrived in the mail from him every week. My mom remembers with particular fondness one about a baseball pitcher who had one arm. *Don't treat her like she's different,* Papa would write on little notes with the articles.

"Well," Mom continued, watching me stand atop the counter, "we're out of cereal, and some other stuff, too. Let's go to the grocery store."

I hopped down with a big smile, because going to the grocery store meant doing what none of my other friends could: riding my bike up and down the aisles. It was an activity that made me feel very, very privileged.

My mother didn't treat the bike like any sort of treat. It was simply a functional choice, like many of the decisions she made so matter-of-factly for me. I couldn't walk long distances, so I rode.

Our local grocery store, Phillip's Market, wasn't nearly as big as the Harris Teeters of today. We had the same shopping route through the small grocery store each time. I'd pedal my pink bike past the Kool-Aid, the Coke, and the little plastic barrels of rainbow-colored drinks, eagerly reaching for them. "They're nothing but sugar water," Mom would say, guiding me away. I always hoped that she'd change her mind on our next shopping trip.

Occasionally, as I casually steered my way through the store, I'd get an awkward look from another shopper. I figured they were jealous of my little white basket and colorful streamers when they had to use rusted gray metal carts. I had a legitimate mission ahead of me: to seek out and knock all the cookies I could reach into my basket.

"Don't go too far," Mom ordered as I slowly pedaled away from her side. She was busy in the boring vegetable aisle, stuffing broccoli and carrots into clear plastic bags.

"I won't. I want to go just over there," I told her as I bounced on my bike seat and pointed to the next aisle over. Mom nodded and gave me the okay sign with her fingers.

I pressed firmly on the orange wood blocks that my dad had cut and secured tightly atop the pedals with black thick rubber bands. My legs were too short to pedal otherwise.

Perusing the aisle, I made a mental checklist of everything I liked before narrowing down the list to Oreos, chewy oatmeal, double chocolate chunk, and ladyfingers. They all tasted great with the milk my mom left for me on the bottom shelf of the refrigerator in a cup with a special plastic lid. The cookies also served as delicious decorations on the little carousel in the kitchen that Mom called a lazy Susan. Just as I was ready to start filling up my basket, I ran into some opposition.

An older woman, an unfriendly schoolmarm type with tightly wound gray curls and an equally stiff and curled upper lip, stood beside me. She narrowed her eyes and grumbled something that I couldn't make out. But I got the gist of her gripe—her tone spoke volumes.

"Awful. Just awful," she then said, peering down at me. I shrank away and felt scared, worried that I might get kicked out of the store altogether. As quickly as I could, I whipped my bike around. My training wheels wobbled back and forth off the ground as I made the sharp turn to leave the aisle. I didn't say a word. Instead I fell in line by my mom's side.

"Where are your cookies?" she asked.

"I can't get them," I said. I used *that* word. The word I was told by Papa never to say, but I said it anyway: *can't.*

"All right," Mom said, skeptically studying my face. I avoided her eyes.

She kissed my forehead and twirled my ponytail with her fingers. "We'll get some when it's time to pass by there again." I could tell she didn't believe me, but I kept a straight face and pedaled on.

Somewhere between the milk and juice aisles, Mom and I crossed paths with the woman. I made every excuse I could not to go forward, but my mom cornered me.

"All right, what's the problem? Why don't you want to go down this aisle?"

I caved and blurted everything out.

"*Oh?*" Mom said. Her voice had a sense of intrigue, like she hoped the scene would unfold again in her presence. "Don't ever let anyone keep you from doing what you want to do," she ordered me.

Then, without instigating it herself, Mom got what she wanted. The old woman from the cookie aisle walked right up to us.

"Little girls aren't supposed to ride around in stores on their bikes," the woman snapped at my mother in an exaggerated whisper. "This *isn't* a circus."

"Not that it's your business, but I happen to have the permission of the manager for her to ride this bike," Mom began icily, placing a bottle of juice into our cart. Then she stepped in closer and faced the woman head-on.

"Why don't you pay more attention to the crap you're putting in *your* cart rather than what my daughter's doing? Because from the looks of it, honey, you could use a few miles on an exercise bike yourself."

I watched in awe. The lady said nothing. Her grumbling stopped and her eyes, formerly angry little slits, were now wide open. She took a look at her cart, then at me, and then back at my mother. She was silent. Only a squeaky wheel on the old woman's cart made any sound as she turned and left.

My mother held her ground and watched until the woman was fully out of sight. Then she went back to shopping, as if the confrontation were as ordinary as the juice boxes on the shelf. She'd delivered her words to that lady so perfectly. It amazed me.

I sat on my bike with my head held high and my shoulders thrust back, emulating my mother's tough, confident stance. I watched her continue to toss groceries into our cart, feeling larger than life. To hell with what anyone else thought. I wanted to be like her: loved or hated but nothing in between; fearless, independent, and strong.

I couldn't wait to tell my dad what she had done. But the way he looked at adapting to life's challenges was another story entirely.

My father wears his heart on his sleeve, and every time I suffer or struggle, I watch that sleeve get tattered and torn a little bit more. Since the day he reentered my life, he vowed to do everything in his power to keep me from feeling pain. A man of few words with his friends, and even fewer words with his family, my father has a tendency to slouch as he stands, making it appear as though the sky is pushing him closer to the ground, away from his strapping height of six feet tall. His hands are muscular and rough, the utensils of his craft as an artisan and a welder. But my father always considered his most important job to be my protector. In his perfect world, he'd place me inside a glass box on a top shelf and I'd only come down once in a while for dusting. I love him for wanting to keep me so safe, but I have no interest in staying put.

"Let's go to the Fair," he'd suggest on the days that my mother went to work as a registered nurse on the open-heart surgical floor at UMass Medical Center. He loved to take me to our local toy store, and I loved it even more. We did this dozens of times, but every time felt just as special and magical as the last. It was our thing.

But I hated that he wouldn't let me bring my bike, insisting that I ride in the cart instead.

"Why?" I'd whine.

"Because you're not supposed to ride your bike at the Fair," he'd say with a sigh.

"Mom says people should worry about what's in their own basket instead of me on my bike," I pointed out.

"She *would*."

"She did, Daddy. She said it," I said with a teasing grin.

"I wish she wouldn't."

"I'm going to tell her you said that," I said playfully.

"It won't make a difference," Dad replied softly.

He was right. It wouldn't.

As he wheeled the shopping cart down the Fair's aisles, he watched me waddle down the rows and rows of dolls, stopping at one in a big white dress.

"You have that one, don't you?" he asked, nodding to the Barbie that had captivated me.

Her name was Wedding Day Barbie and, to me, she was perfect. Lace and ruffles were delicately draped over her long, plastic legs and her golden hair cascaded down her back underneath a beautiful, delicate veil.

"No, Daddy, I don't have this one. I don't have anything like her!"

"All right, then," he said with a small smile.

He reached for the doll. I could feel my heart thudding with excitement as I watched him place her in the cart. I tried to help, reaching toward her as best I could. But Dad said, "It's easier if I do it."

Still smiling, I followed him down the aisle, walking slowly with my fingers poked through the cart's plastic honeycomb.

Other girls my age had flocked to the Barbie aisle as well. I noticed a few with pretty ribbons in their hair. These little girls came up to their parents' waists, not their thighs, I noticed. Just as I was taking in one girl's long, slim legs, tan from the summer and looking a whole lot like Barbie's, she locked eyes with me. I looked back at her, wondering momentarily whether I should wave hello. Then she pointed at me.

"Why is she so small, Mommy? Is she okay?"

"Don't stare," the girl's mother replied softly.

My dad picked up speed when he noticed the pointing and whispering. He pushed the cart faster and faster down the aisle. It was as if he thought we could outrun the looks and the questions.

"But, Mommy, *why* is she so small?" the girl persisted.

"How about you ride in here for a while?" Dad suggested, gesturing to the cart.

"But, Daddy, I can walk," I said, aware of the little girl's questioning but not overly concerned about it. Her words didn't register with me the way they did with my father.

In one sweeping motion he picked me up anyway and placed me into the cart, guiding me out of the doll aisle. Just before we finished our shopping trip, I was allowed to pick one more item from the hodgepodge section, which we affectionately called the "junk aisle." I snagged a small, multicolored porcelain swan. Dad paid for the toys, smiling as he pushed the cart out to his GMC truck parked in the lot. He had done a good job. He made me smile, bought me toys, and kept me from the stares and pointed fingers as best he could.

"Dad, I'll carry this in the house to show Mom, okay? I wanna show Mommy everything!" I squealed, holding the bag up in the air.

"No, pumpkin. It's easier if I do it."

That night, my dad and I shared our usual post-bath-time ritual. I sat in our yellow tub until my little hands and tiny toes turned into prunes. The swan sat beside the sink. When the bathwater grew lukewarm, Dad would always help me out. The tub was far too deep for me to get out of with my stubby legs, but with him, I never worried about slipping on the wet tile—my biggest fear. He was always there to wrap me in a towel and lift me directly from the water to the counter to dry off.

When he was sure that I was secure and wrapped up tight, he'd crouch down to open the cabinet and take out his massive silver hair dryer with a shiny pearl handle. We named it Silverado.

Silverado always excited me and made me laugh. The air roared out with such force! My thick brown hair blew back as if I was facing a hurricane and my eyelashes barely hung on to my eyelids. And when it was all over, Dad would run his fingers across my head, making sure it was completely dry. "There," he always said softly. "How's that?"

In those days we didn't think about what would happen when I turned sixteen, or eighteen, or twenty-one. Neither of us thought about the fact that one day I would get older and want different things out of life.

Back then I was just his pumpkin pie.

Even when I faced a real problem at school due to my size, I still didn't think of myself as different, or worse, as a dwarf. No one used that word with me. No one ever called me that or discussed my "condition" with me. I was just Tiffanie.

Then, in first grade, I got stuck. Suddenly, just being Tiffanie wasn't enough.

Douglas Elementary School was a big place, considering the small town it served. There were two major hallways and a large gym. What I remember most is the bathroom and its dark blue and gray walls. It had two sinks and three stalls. There was one wastepaper basket, two soap dispensers, and one paper towel holder. It's funny how certain childhood details stick inside your brain like chewing gum stuck to a desk at school.

One afternoon, I excused myself from my first-grade class and ended up getting trapped for what felt like hours on the other side of that bathroom door. In reality, I'm aware that it couldn't have been longer than about fifteen minutes. In my young mind, though, it felt like days.

The weight and imposing presence of a heavy fire door makes it a monstrous and impenetrable object to a handicapped child. It's more than just a door. It's the difference between freedom and imprisonment.

On this particular day, unlike others—when a teacher followed me, opened the heavy door, and waited—I followed a friend and entered the girls' room, armed with my reach tool. Afterward, my friend flushed and left for class, and I couldn't let myself out. The door was too heavy to pull and the handle was too high for me to get a proper grip.

I was trapped.

Weaponless and anxious, I waited for someone to rescue me. With my back to the wall, I slid down to the floor. I felt grainy bits of dirt under my fingertips as I started to cry.

I knew something was not right. It was the first time I remember feeling different, even if I didn't understand why.

Was it because I wasn't allowed Kool-Aid? I wondered. Most of the other kids had Kool-Aid for lunch, but I never convinced my mom to buy some. It was just 100 percent juice for me.

Maybe the Kool-Aid had something to do with why I was different, I thought to myself. What if I could fix everything by guzzling Kool-Aid by the gallon? Maybe that was the key!

It was a childish, magical solution to a problem I didn't fully understand—the best connection I could make while growing up ignorant of my disability.

My mom had told me I'd be tested in life, and that not everything would be easy for me. I would have to fight for what I wanted, but that was normal, she said. It wasn't until I sat on the floor in the blue and gray girls' room that I wondered, *why* wasn't this normal for other kids? I'd never heard of *them* getting stuck in the bathroom. Why was I the only one?

I brushed the dirt off my hands and looked around the room for a tool, a weapon, a solution. There was nothing.

I knew I'd get out at some point, but what if this happened again? Would I ever be able to drink enough Kool-Aid to prevent this from occurring a second time?

Eventually someone came looking for me. I made it out of the bathroom and back to my class. The following day, swiftly and without any fuss, Dad took care of the problem for me. He swooped in to Douglas Elementary to install additional locks and door handles about a foot beneath the existing ones, so I could use the girls' bathroom on my own. And he did it without a word to anyone. Not my mom. Not the school. He didn't even ask for permission first.

He just did it.

I remember a teacher once asking each kid in my class, "What does your daddy do for a living?"

My response? "He fixes things."

# CHAPTER 3

# Everyone Has Problems

With a friend at my
preschool graduation, c. 1986.

Throughout my childhood, I treasured my stuffed animal collection. It grew larger after every bone-corrective surgery. One of my other favorite (if less traditional) playthings was my dad's antique Pioneer stereo, which he bought in 1972. The behemoth system seemed to take up half our small, one-window living room. I was mesmerized by it. The base system, tuner, and equalizer were stacked on top of one another, layered like metal cakes, and it had reel-to-reel, a cassette deck, a turntable, and a radio. The entire thing towered over me. At seven years old, most things did.

Beneath the stereo system, piles of colorful square sleeves with big round records tucked inside stood against the wall. A pair of white bubble headphones slept on top of the stack, its wire coiled neatly underneath it. Dad liked to play the Beatles and the band America, but the album I heard most was *Fiddler on the Roof.*

In the evenings when he came home from work, he'd make himself a rum and Coke and sing along to "If I Were a Rich Man" as he relaxed in our blue recliner, shoes kicked off, toes tapping along to the beat. I didn't understand the lyrics, but I knew it made him happy to watch me twirl around the living room and sing along, too.

Beginning in 1969, my father worked in Worcester in the sheet metal fabrication department at Norton Company, a factory that produces grinding wheels, silicon carbide, and coated and bonded abrasives. He always liked his job.

"You'll never believe what this guy Jimmy did," he'd say to my mom after work. "He took one of the bulletproof Apache helicopter seats we produced and said he was going to use it for his go-cart. Can you believe that? Pretty cool idea."

Always the class clown growing up in a very strict Catholic school, Dad tried to find humor in every situation. There was always a story to tell after his shift, and I never saw him come home upset. His hours at Norton weren't insufferable, and the job didn't interfere with the nighttime jewelry-making courses he loved so much. One evening when he got home, Dad poured his usual into a tumbler glass and settled in the living room. "Look what I made for Mom," he said, pulling a domed, heart-shaped ring out of his pocket to show me. I loved shiny things and anything that sparkled.

The ring was solid rose gold and reminded me of a full moon. Half of the heart was smooth, while the other half was carved with deep ridges. He smiled at my wide-eyed reaction. Time after time, my father proved he could make anything with his two hands. I envisioned him constructing valuable, one-of-a-kind trinkets inside a vaulted room lined with drawers filled with rubies, diamonds, emeralds, and sheets of gold. One day when my surgeries were over, I thought, he'd bring me there.

"Let's give it to Mom," he said, tucking the ring back into his pocket. I followed him out of the living room, through our tiny dining room, and into our even smaller kitchen. It was a cozy room, with white walls, dark brown cabinets, and a single blue curtain on the window above the sink. It took me a while to catch up to people as they walked through our house, and I was endlessly impressed at how fast my dad could get from one room to another. I watched as he gave my mom a kiss, then the heart-shaped ring. She wrapped her arms around him and kissed him back. "Thank you, dear!" she squealed. I had no idea they were still divorced. They would never officially get remarried.

My eighth birthday was just a few weeks away. Maybe I'd get to wear this new heart ring, I thought, the air catching in my throat and making a soft whistling sound as I imagined this exciting possibility. Or, even better, maybe my dad would make me one of my own.

After dinner that night, I followed him down to the basement to give our German shepherd, Bruiser, the leftovers from our meal. Of all the rooms in our house, Bruiser loved the basement most of all. The floor was cool against his thick fur, making it an ideal sleeping spot. And if he got cold, he'd curl up on the big plaid dog bed by the furnace. Hanging out in the basement also allowed him to play watchdog. But Bruiser was more interested in watching me than keeping an eye out for intruders.

For as long as we had our loyal shepherd, he would never let me near the basement staircase unless Dad was with me. The stairs, easily manageable for my parents, remained a steep, dan-

gerous slope to me. I was scolded each time I approached them on
my own and had fallen down them too many times to count. It
gave Mom nightmares, but their threats never stopped me. They
made me more determined to find a way—my way—to conquer
them. One day I wouldn't have to sink down to the floor and de-
scend the stairs on my behind. One day, Bruiser wouldn't need to
protect me with a well-meaning shove away from them. I'd be able
to do it on my own.

"I'm off," Mom announced, coming down to the basement to
meet us. It was just before seven p.m., and her night shift was
about to start. I'd see her again at five in the morning when Dad
would bring me to her at the hospital and then leave for Norton
Company. She gave me a big hug and a kiss, lifting me off the
cellar floor and then placing me back down. She smelled of White
Shoulders perfume and Suave shampoo.

"See you in the morning, honey bunny," she said to me before
she hugged Dad, squeezed Bruiser's ears, and went outside and got
into her Pontiac Bonneville (we called her Bonnie). The heart
ring glistened on her finger.

Back upstairs, Dad relaxed with his drink while the Pioneer system played its usual tunes. With a Cabbage Patch doll tucked tightly
under my arm, I snuck into Mom's bedroom. Then I pulled out
the bottom drawers of her dresser to make a ladder and climbed
to the top of her bureau. From up on my perch, I flipped open her
glittery gold jewelry box to reveal her long, beaded necklaces. My
arms were too short to fasten a regular one around my neck, but I
could whip the beads over my head to put them on. I entertained
myself until bedtime with a solo fashion show.

"Pay attention to your *own* cart," I said into the mirror, imitating my mom with a big smile.

On other afternoons, when the *Fiddler on the Roof* record was returned to its sleeve, it was my turn to play music in the living room. Of all my tapes, Cyndi Lauper was my favorite. Ruby, my imaginary friend (named after my mom's jewels), loved music just as much as I did.

"Let's play Cyndi," Ruby would suggest. "Let's dance."

Of course, I couldn't reach the stereo buttons, but there were ways around this.

Though my feet were tiny, I knew that it would be too much of a gamble to stand on top of the pile of records—I imagined them smashing into tiny, jagged pieces under my weight, so I didn't take the chance. Instead, I stood atop our extra-large lobster pot and reached carefully to work the buttons of the cassette player. Balancing on my makeshift stool, I envisioned Cyndi coming to my eighth birthday party, surprising my friends.

I had lots of friends—real ones—but my closest friend was Katie Duso. She had brown hair like me, a lisp, and wide-set, oblong brown eyes. Katie was more of a tomboy than a girly girl, and we got along well. She helped me reach the art supplies at school and walked beside me like a bodyguard in the hallway so I wouldn't get trampled.

My half brother, Nicolas (from my dad's first marriage), didn't need a bodyguard. He could reach everything he wanted, including Dad's system. He didn't need to slide down the stairs when he visited on weekends. He could run down them and back up again in a flash. Nicolas had a full head of curly brown hair, small freckles across the bridge of his nose, and a gap between his two front teeth. He was an athletic kid, two years older than me, and I watched him accomplish everyday tasks with ease. It never dawned on me that things were difficult for me and easy for Nick because I was handicapped and he was not.

Nick never treated me like I was different, either. Together we'd park ourselves in front of the TV and watch WWF and then reenact the tag team matches with our pillows. The typical younger sister, I wanted to do everything he did, and I begged him to help me make forts out of sheets and the dining room chairs. I chalked up our differences to his age and the fact that he was a boy. One day, I figured, I would be that age, too, and prove girls could do everything just like the boys.

On many a weekday afternoon, I had doctors' appointments at Children's Hospital Boston. And doctors' appointments often meant preparation for more surgeries. They were as normal as brushing my teeth. I had no idea that other girls my age didn't visit the doctor as regularly as I did. Nor did I realize that my doctors' appointments were nothing like my friends' appointments when they got a cold or strep throat.

In school, there was one other girl who talked about having surgery. She, like the rest of the kids in my class, sat in a glossy, colored chair. Mine was just thick, plain wood, and it was modified, as was my desk, to sit very close to the ground. I peered up at her, feeling like I was practically sitting on the classroom floor. I was so envious of her desk and that shiny red chair.

Turned out, she had something else I wanted, too—her tonsils removed. It was nothing, she explained to me, and the best part was that afterward, she could have all the ice cream and Popsicles that her stomach could handle. She started the Tonsil Club shortly after, but I couldn't belong because I hadn't had mine removed. I longed to have that operation. It was not unlike when the newest Barbie came out. If other girls had it, I wanted it, too. But my tonsils stayed in my throat, and instead of ice cream, I had crushed ice with ginger ale after every operation, working my way up to Campbell's chicken noodle soup. Even though I was left out of the Tonsil Club, I was very much included with the "normal" kids in elementary school.

"Why are you small?" I'd get asked once in a while.

"I don't know. Why are you tall?" I'd reply with a shrug of my shoulders. And that was that. I was smaller and they were taller. It was what it was. I remember other kids getting teased in school for various reasons, though I actually never suffered the same fate. But my classmates did notice something unusual about me: I didn't look like the rest of my family.

"Are you adopted?" a girl named Mandy asked me innocently one day in school.

"I don't know," I began. "What does that mean?"

"It means that your mom and dad aren't your real mom and dad," she explained. "I think you're adopted. You have a different mommy and daddy somewhere, because you don't look like the ones you live with. They're so much taller than you," Mandy continued.

My stomach felt like it was twisting into knots. *Not my real mom and dad? Will I have to move in with new parents somewhere else?* Images of being lost and alone, like Bambi in the woods, bombarded my imagination. I couldn't shake my panicked feeling all morning, so over lunch I asked Katie if she also thought I was adopted.

"I don't know," she replied simply.

"Do I look like my mom and dad?" I pressed on. "What about Nick—do I look like him?"

Katie shrugged. "Maybe Nick knows if you're adopted. You should ask him."

Her answer gave me enough solace to get through the rest of my day. If I were truly adopted, I figured, surely he would have told me. Every weekend when Dad would pick Nick up, we'd play and laugh, and not a single word was whispered about adoption.

"If you were adopted, there would be papers. A certificate," Nick said after I told him what had happened at school. He barely looked away from his Nintendo game flashing on the TV. "We can look around. If we find a certificate, then you're adopted," he added, pausing the game.

While Mom prepared dinner and Dad let Bruiser out, Nick and I made our way to the spare bedroom down the hall that Mom used for her sewing. She always kept the door shut, and the handle was too high above my head to reach, which created an air of mystery about what was on the other side. But Nick was able to open it for us. Looking past the piles of fabric and sewing supplies, we focused on a tall shelving unit loaded with odds and ends that didn't seem to belong anywhere else in the house. I worried that maybe I didn't belong, either.

"I'll start here," Nick said, pulling a gold and brown tin box down from a high shelf. He popped open the lid but found nothing but spools of thread, buttons, and scissors.

I removed each book off the bottom two shelves and sat on the floor.

"Be sure to look at every page," he ordered. "A certificate could be stuck between the pages." He peered inside straw baskets and took a few more off the shelf and set them aside. Then he grabbed a folder balanced on top of some clothing patterns, sending the whole pile toppling to the floor. Everything scattered across the rug, including a single piece of paper with a fancy green design adorning the border. Nick reached for it and my heart pounded in my chest. It was covered in bold, typed letters; a round, gold seal; and official-looking stamps.

"What is it?" I asked anxiously. "What do you have?"

He held it close and just looked at me. "A certificate."

"Read it to me," I demanded. "Please!"

"No," he said. "I don't want to."

My eyes brimmed with tears as I grabbed wildly at the paper, but Nick put his hand on my forehead and held the sheet behind him, keeping it far out of my grasp. After fighting him for a moment, I knew what I had to do. I left the spare bedroom and walked down the hallway toward the kitchen. It felt like time had stopped as I approached my mother.

"Mommy?" I said in the smallest voice, standing by the refrigerator.

"Yes, honey?" she replied while stirring a pot on the stove.

"Are you happy about me?"

She dropped her wooden spoon, which landed with a *clank* on the side of the metal pot. Then she spun around to face me and dropped to her knees.

"Oh my God," she said, picking me up and holding me in her arms. "You are the *best* thing to ever happen to me. Of course I'm happy about you!" she said, squeezing me tighter. I felt her chest heave and heard her sniffle. "Of *course* I'm happy about you," she repeated. Then she let me go and looked into my eyes. I watched as tears ran down her cheeks. It made me want to cry, too. "I love you more than all the stars in the sky. What would ever make you ask such a question?"

I didn't know what to say.

"Why would you ask me this?" she asked again.

Still, I remained silent. I shrugged and squeezed my small arms as tight as they could get around her. I wasn't expecting her reaction and all I wanted to do was hug her, feeling comforted by the warmth of her body and the sweet smell of her perfume. I stopped worrying about being adopted and took a deep breath, feeling like maybe it was all just a big mistake.

"You may be little, you may be short, but I love you, because you're mine," she said, continuing to hold me. "You're *mine*. Always remember that." And I believed her.

That night, I slept soundly under the tent Nick and I made together, and things went back to normal over the weekend.

On Monday, I didn't have the chance to tell Mandy I wasn't adopted after all because Mom kept me home from school. I missed a lot of school due to my doctors' appointments and surgeries. But on the days that I didn't get to see my friends, Ruby would appear.

"Play Cyndi," she said, motioning to the play button on the Pioneer system. I hummed "Girls Just Wanna Have Fun" in anticipation as the tiny wheels in the tape began to turn. I was wearing my mom's jewelry again, feeling confident that I looked a lot like her. The domed heart ring turned circles around my tiny finger and her long, beaded necklaces swayed from side to side as I shimmied atop the lobster pot.

Before Cyndi could begin singing, Mom was standing over me, holding the very certificate Nick had found. She turned the music off with a flick of her long, salmon pink fingernail and tossed her feathered, blond Farrah Fawcett–style hair.

"Why was this in your room?" Mom asked. She looked very confused. "This belongs to my sewing machine, Tiffie. If I lose it and something happens to my machine I can't get it replaced."

I felt a rush of relief and a twinge of embarrassment.

"I don't want you going through my sewing room," she continued. "There are pins and needles and scissors in there. You could get hurt. Promise me you will stay out of that room."

"I promise!" I shouted happily. "I love you."

"I love you, too! Now, it's really time to go," she said, motioning for me to hand over her jewelry. "We're going to be late for your doctor's appointment, sweetheart." I wiggled out of the necklaces, my hair falling into my eyes as I pulled them over my head.

On our way to the hospital that afternoon, Mom and I bopped

along to my Cyndi cassette. The volume was turned up obnoxiously high and I made sure to sing along extra loud. Our time together in the car made the exhausting trip to Boston fun. It was a mini party in her car.

Compared to our very small bedroom town of Douglas, Boston seemed like the land of endless possibilities. It was intriguing. Even if all I knew of the city existed between the walls of the hospital's orthopedic ward, to me it was like the Land of Oz. It took forever to get there, but the huge silver skyscrapers and the cars, trucks, and ambulances that whizzed past us always enchanted me. Clusters of people maneuvered up and down the skinny streets, drivers blew their horns constantly, and my mom cursed at the ones that cut in front of our car.

In my imagination, the people who sat up above our car in glass boxes—Mom called them tollbooth operators—protected the city.

"Jesus Christ," she hissed as she handed over money through her window.

The tollbooth operator was expressionless and stood perfectly still with his hand outstretched.

"Soon we won't have a pot to piss in if you keep raising the prices."

After the hassle of the tollbooths, parking was the biggest challenge. We'd circle around and around trying to find a spot. Eventually it became a game. Who could spot an open space first? The way I had it figured out, if the operator at the gate was nice, the parking gods would be, too. If he was grumpy, we'd spend at least forty-five minutes hunting for a space. On this trip to the hospital, because I was already happy from dancing to Cyndi, I made sure to wave and smile at the tollbooth operator. And, *poof!* We got our best parking spot to date, right in front.

Mom and I made our way through the wide corridors of the massive hospital, much of which was worn, faded, discolored, and drab. I never liked the furniture inside Boston's Children's Hospital. Furniture always made a big impression on me since chairs and tables were usually right at eye level. The hospital wood seemed too pale, as if it were sick. But I wasn't sick. I was there to look at my bones on X-rays, to make sure they were straight and strong. I was also there to pick out a stuffed animal from the gift shop. Other kids didn't have animals to accompany them down the halls or in their beds. Instead, they had tubes and wires with them, and mounds of blankets covering up their bodies. Some kids couldn't sit up. They'd lie there, tired, sad, and scared, while their moms or dads hovered over them, wiping away their tears. I wasn't allowed to cower like they did.

"Everyone has problems; everyone has pain," Mom would say to me during any moments of weakness. "Some you see and some you don't see. But it's there and crying doesn't make it go away."

That made me wonder what my mom suffered from. What was her pain? I wanted to handle my pain the same way she did— with ease, as though it almost didn't exist at all.

As we walked down the long corridor toward Dr. Shapiro's office, the lights above our heads cast a yellowish glow. Strange artwork dotted the walls throughout the hallways and waiting rooms. One painting in my doctor's office always scared me. It was mostly an abstract, blotchy mess, but in the middle, there was a boy swimming in the ocean. He was raising his arm up out of the waves, but it was a frighteningly odd shape—like it had been badly broken in the surf. No one else seemed to be scared by it. But seeing it meant I was closer to yet another surgery, so it made my heart thump harder. Surgery meant that anesthesia, tubes, wires, big beeping machines, needles, and rubbing alcohol were on their way. I'd squeeze my animal tighter when I saw that paint-ing, burying my face in its soft little head.

From keeping my legs straight to correcting my clubbed feet to closing a small cleft in the soft palate of my mouth, I'd had liter-ally dozens of surgeries since I was ten months old, and I'd battled arthritis for as long as I could remember. That's the nature of the beast that is diastrophic dysplasia. But from what I gathered from the adult conversations, this next surgery would be a more com-plicated series of procedures aimed to make me more indepen-dent. And it would be nothing like what I'd been through before.

The surgery coming up was more than the typical osteotomy to correct the irregular joints of my legs—a procedure I was used to and didn't even really mind. I actually enjoyed the hard casts woven around my legs when I woke up. I could draw on them as much as I wanted. Mom made sure I never ran out of markers, stencils, and stickers for decorating the white plaster.

Months earlier, my mother had watched a series on the news about a radical new procedure called bone lengthening. It was used to correct uneven limbs, and one doctor was performing the surgery as a way to lengthen the limbs of children with dwarfism.

The procedure promised the potential for great results, but it was—it is—a grueling, painful process. In order to lengthen a bone, surgeons first cut the bone in half. Then they drill a thick stainless steel pin into each side of the broken bone and attach an external fixator. A week after surgery, the patient begins turning the pins four times a day (one-quarter millimeter each time) to achieve one millimeter in length between the broken bones daily. The hope is that, as the bone is stretched apart, the body will fill in the gap with new bone, thus adding length. When the patient wakes up from the surgery, the pins protrude from the limb, which is encased in a metal halo to keep it stable. The sight of a patient undergoing bone lengthening is a hard one to bear, even for a mother as tough as mine.

Curious and inspired by the procedure and passionate about helping me live as normal a life as possible, Mom called Dr. Fred E. Shapiro. He was a little man who wore rimless oval glasses, a navy blue blazer, and a tie. It was a big deal to my mom that he taught at Harvard Medical School, and an even bigger deal that she trusted him. He was sweet, soft-spoken, and brilliant. Occasionally, he even made a joke. He had been my orthopedic surgeon since I was a baby, and I grew to love him as an important adult in my life.

But in this conversation between my mom and Dr. Shapiro, there was almost nothing I could relate to—nor could I understand much of what they said. No one smiled. Everything was serious as they studied X-rays of my legs. Dr. Shapiro moved his pen vertically and then horizontally against the images of my bones. He was explaining something I couldn't comprehend and he used words that I had never heard before, like "pin care" and "consolidation" and "angulation." But I could make out that this surgery would take longer, be more painful, and generally be a bigger deal.

While Mom was digesting the information, I began to get bored.

"My birthday is coming up," I interjected as they spoke, searching Dr. Shapiro's face for that comforting smile. "We're going to have pizza!"

Dr. Shapiro glanced in my direction, nodded, and lifted a finger to indicate that he'd speak to me in just a minute.

"There's a window of opportunity," he told my mother. "You can have it done twice, if you decide to do so, between the ages of eight and twenty."

"So if she wanted to do it a second time she'd be in her teens." Mom paused, then looked at me with a small smile. "She could decide for herself then if it's worth it."

Dr. Shapiro nodded.

I loved it when I heard my mom say things like, "She can decide for herself." I loved having any chance to make my mom proud.

"We would strive for two inches in her tibias first, then two inches in her femurs for a total of four inches. It's the recommended amount," Dr. Shapiro concluded.

One night not long after my appointment, I heard Mom explaining the surgery to my dad as I played with my Barbies.

"No, no, no," I heard Dad say. "More surgery? It's never ending."

Mom kept speaking over him, using some of the big words I'd heard in Dr. Shapiro's office.

Then Dad left and went downstairs to see Bruiser. I heard the cellar door shut, then Mom appeared quietly in my doorway. I brushed the knotted hair of my doll and dressed her in a sequined outfit.

"Tiffie," she began, "would you like to do more things on your own without the help of Mommy or Daddy?"

"I already do things on my own."

"You do things with books and tools," she said, sitting down next to me. "Would you like to do things without those?"

I nodded my head, thinking about all the books I had to slide across the floor to reach the Pioneer system. It was pretty tiring.

"I don't like my chair at school," I replied. "It's ugly."

"I know. I know you'd like to sit in a chair like your friends and like Mom and Dad. What about the doorknobs? Would you like to reach those, too?"

"You and Daddy do that."

"But we won't always be around to help you. You should want to do it yourself."

That worried me. Where were they going? I smiled anyway and nodded.

It was decided. I would undergo the bone-lengthening surgery.

•◆•

The morning of my operation, Dad woke me up. As my eyes adjusted to the light coming in through my window, I noticed something fluffy and white on my bed.

It was a new stuffed animal, bigger than all the others from my previous surgeries combined.

"I'll see you when you wake up," Dad said softly, patting the giant white polar bear with brown eyes and happy grin. "Until then, he'll be by your side."

"Can I name him Frosty?" I asked.

"Frosty is a snowman."

"This Frosty is better. He won't melt."

"All right. Call him Frosty."

"Daddy, are you okay?" I asked, sitting up to look at him.

"Oh, sure," he said. "I'm fine." I could tell he wasn't. "Mom just makes too many decisions without me. But you don't think about that. You think about presents after surgery."

"Mom says I won't need so much help after this one," I told him. "She says I won't need so many tools."

"She's right," he said, nodding. "She's right." He repeated it as though he were trying to convince himself that this surgery was worth it.

"I'd like to reach more stuff," I continued. "If I can reach the stereo without my tools, will you let me play Cyndi whenever I want?"

"Maybe we'll even get you your own stereo," he said with a smile.

"A pink one! A boom box like Barbie's!" I yelled.

"All right. We'll see what the Fair has for boom boxes."

"I think Mom made a good decision then, Dad. Don't worry."

The truth was, Dad always worried. So did Mom, but she was better at hiding her emotions.

In our rush out the door to get to the hospital, we forgot my Cyndi tape. The drive went by fast but it was hardly the party it had been on previous drives. Frosty sat in the back with Mom's bag, which she'd packed with pajamas and other necessities. She never left my side during any surgery. I carried Chester the cat, one of my favorite animals, under my arm, and I studied Mom's expression as she drove and saw not an ounce of weakness or regret. Her confidence gave me comfort.

Moments before we pulled into the Children's parking lot, Mom explained to me again, in the simplest manner, that this surgery was part of a bigger picture. The bone-lengthening operation was part of my ongoing fight to do things on my own, she said. I was still confused. I told her I felt like I was already doing things on my own.

"Without tools, honey bunny. You will be able to do so much more without using your tools. Mommy and Daddy won't always be around to help you," she said.

Now I was even more scared. Why was she saying this again? Where were they going that I couldn't go, too? I didn't want to be away from them. I wanted to have them forever and I wondered if having surgery to be more independent would make them go away somehow. The thought frightened me so much that from that point on, I promised myself to never watch *Bambi* or any other Disney movie where the mom dies.

When we arrived at pre-op, a familiar place, a man in blue scrubs and a Disney net hat lowered my hospital bed. Already in a gown, I pulled the warm white blankets over me. They felt like they were fresh out of the dryer.

Mom squeezed my hand and I watched a nurse wheel a massive machine toward me with a rubber mask and a long tube attached.

"Take a few deep breaths," a doctor told me. He assured me that the mask would smell like juicy citrus.

It smelled of rotting oranges.

"Wait, wait, wait," I pleaded. The sense of losing control made me panic. I had to submit and I hated it. I couldn't stand the mask, but I had endured it before because the needle and IV were far worse. The mask gave me a way to be put under and then wake up with an IV in my hand instead of the other way around. I had to pick my poison, but I wished there were a third option. The surgery itself never fazed me. It was the fall down the rabbit hole I feared.

"C'mon, Tiffie," Mom said. "You know you have to have it. There's no time to wait."

"Can I hold the mask?" I begged. I needed the sense, even if it was a false one, to be in control of what was happening.

Mom asked the anesthesiologist to give me the mask. His eyebrows drew together. He wasn't accustomed to granting such a request, but he complied.

I took the mask in my hand—it looked like a misshapen mushroom. Then I took a deep breath. Everything around me slowed down, and all the people and machines seemed to be floating around the room. Faces became blotchy like the painting in Dr. Shapiro's office. Voices started to echo and slur. Out of the corner of my eye, I saw Mom take Frosty out of my bed.

I thought of the movie *Alice in Wonderland*. It was like I was taking one of her pills, the red one, and it would make me taller. But I knew this wouldn't be nearly as painless as what Alice went through.

I inhaled again. The hallway tunneled and went dark around the edges. I felt like I was falling. Nurses and doctors began to wheel my bed toward the operating room. I heard Mom somewhere in the background tell me she loved me. With my free hand I motioned for my cat with the cute white belly. I wasn't prepared to let him go yet. He had a crooked smile, which I loved, and his black whiskers curled like a second grin around his big, round cheeks. I traced the outline of his whiskers, finally feeling like it would all be okay.

# CHAPTER 4

# Toughening Up

An elementary school portrait.

A week after surgery, I was home, but everything felt different. Sleeping was difficult. I was constantly jolted awake by tremors in my shins. A sliver of daylight was shining through my mom's bedroom window and directly into my eyes. All I wanted to do was stay in bed—specifically my mom's. Her bedroom was always so peaceful and comforting to me that it became my recovery room when I came home. Maybe it was the lilac wallpaper or the flowery scent of her White Shoulders perfume, but something about her room just felt safe. Dad came over every day, but rarely stayed the night. Still mending his relationship with my mom after the divorce, he would continue living in his Webster apartment for the next several years.

That first afternoon home, Mom made cinnamon buns, but my pain medication smothered my appetite. I'd slept through breakfast, and lunch was approaching. The whole house smelled of sugar, and my sensory memory of rotting citrus drifted away.

I was eight years old and the height of a toddler. But that was about to change.

As I snuggled underneath the fluffy comforter with stacks of pillows tucked between my body and the solid oak headboard, Mom entered with a smile and two plates, each with a giant cinnamon bun. She pushed Frosty and Chester aside (someone had tucked them in next to me while I slept) and sat beside me on her bed.

"Try to pick at it, honey bunny," she said.

As I toyed with the frosting and forced a few bites down, Mom reached over to her bedside table and grabbed a handful of papers, a glue stick, and photos—mostly of me—and set them down in her lap. With the glue stick between her fingers, she thumbed through the pages, reading what she had previously jotted down in the margins. I recognized the thick black lettering stamped on each sheet—they came from my Papa's big green typewriter.

On countless visits to my grandfather's house, we would find him at the kitchen table, pounding away on his typewriter, stamping out his words on thick white paper. He wrote a sports column at the *Middlesex News*. I hoped that one day I could be a writer, too. I wanted to sit at a typewriter (a pink one, ideally), making my own words appear on the page, pausing at the end of each line before concluding, "That's good," just as Papa did.

"This is your story," Mom told me as she rubbed glue across the backs of the photos I had selected and pressed them down firmly on the pages. Naturally, I picked the shots where I was wearing outfits that I deemed complete and perfect in every way, with matching necklaces and rings.

I felt annoyed that I didn't have a say in choosing the words. I wanted to create my own story.

And my story would *definitely* be different from the one my mom wrote about me.

*This project is dedicated to my daughter, Tiffanie, who was born with diastrophic dysplasia. It is through her pain and suffering that I have learned so much about this syndrome and the rehabilitation process. Through it all, she has maintained her zest for life and is truly my inspiration.*

My understanding of diastrophic dysplasia—two words that I could barely pronounce, let alone comprehend—grew little by little as time ticked by with the external fixators drilled into my legs. They were quite dramatic-looking devices, with thick metal bars attached to my shins to stabilize the pins inside my bones. I was beginning to associate my short stature with my surgeries.

At night, the tremors in my shins grew worse. Each time they struck, they were relentless. I tried to will them to stop and hoped they'd dull to nothing, as they eventually did with medication. I focused on the thick, plastic blinds pulled shut across the sliding glass doors of Mom's bedroom that led out to our deck. For just a moment, I had peace.

One night, when I was wondering when I'd be able to go outside next, I heard voices downstairs growing louder and louder.

"Don't you make *me* out to be the monster," Mom barked. "Don't you fucking dare!" She fired an arsenal of four-letter words at my dad, who sounded sadder in his response.

"I didn't know her surgery would be like this. You didn't tell me!"

"Like what?"

"Like *this*!" His volume rose to match my mom's.

"Painful?"

"Yes! She just had her eighth birthday party and now she's stuck in a room and can barely sit up."

Without warning, the tremor grew stronger, angrier, shaking the muscles in my calves. Pain developed in my ankles and rapidly intensified, right along with my parents' argument.

"Life is painful, Gerry. Diastrophic dysplasia is painful! When are you going to accept that? It's painful for me to put her through surgery time after time to correct her bones. It was painful for me to hear she got trapped in a bathroom for God knows how long!"

"I fixed the school bathroom," Dad interrupted.

"It's not about the school, it's about her life! I want more for her life! I don't ever want her to feel stuck again because we're not around."

"I'll be around. I'll take care of her!"

"Jesus Christ, Gerry. What are you going to do, follow her around until she's an old lady, placing locks and handles on all the doors she can't reach?"

"Yes!"

"*No*, you *won't*."

"The bottom line is, you didn't tell me it would be like this!" Dad shouted, now just as loud as Mom.

"I did tell you. You didn't listen. So I made the choice."

"*You* made the choice?"

"Someone has to. I don't want her to have to suck up to a caregiver all her life because she can't do something herself. Is that what you want? Do you know how many people get abused because of their handicap?"

What's a caregiver? I wondered. I'd heard the word "handicap" before, but I couldn't remember where. Did it have something to do with where we parked our car? The pain roared back, silencing my thoughts. It grew more explosive by the second, vibrating inside me like a threatening volcano.

"You know it all, then. You're the all-knowing Robin."

"I know what it's like to fight. I know what battles she has ahead of her. Her fight with this condition has only begun and it will only get worse."

Mom had been reading all about diastrophic dysplasia since she learned of my diagnosis. It worsens with time, damaging cartilage, hampering bone development, and causing joint deformities called contractures, which confine movement. I was destined for a wheelchair if I didn't consistently exercise, strengthen, and stretch.

"She's going to hate you," Dad shouted. "When she gets older, all the exercising you forced her to do will make her hate you."

"Then let her hate me."

To Mom, the chance for me to live independently was too important to compromise—and she would fight like hell to help me do it. For Dad, the end did not justify the means. I just wanted the pain and the arguing to stop. I couldn't take it anymore. From deep inside, I let out the loudest scream I could muster.

Dad was the first to come through the door. Mom was right behind him, ready to help quiet the pain and tremors with another scheduled dose of pain medication. My mother reacted while my father comforted, making his way over to the edge of the bed to sit beside me. Remnants of their dispute lingered in his eyes. If looks could kill, his would have strangled my mom. He hated my surgeries and he hated how accepting Mom was of them—and how accepting I had become of surgery, too. I could read it all over his face.

I squeezed my eyes shut and swallowed two chalky pills. Gently, Dad pulled away the sheets and placed a hand over each of my feet, rubbing the tops of them with his coarse fingertips. That soothed everything. The arguing, the pain, it was all gone, at least for now.

"Dad, can you make me an automatic foot-rubbing machine?"

"An automatic foot rubber?" he repeated, stifling a smile. It sounded more like "rubba" when he said it. Dad always had a Bostonian accent, so he occasionally dropped his r's.

"Maybe you can use some of the same metal they put inside me and make fingers that move back and forth," I suggested. "I think you can do it. You can make anything."

"I'll draw up some plans," he replied, humoring me, though I felt quite sure he'd actually get to work on it. Silently, I wished that the pills would kick in sooner.

"I could help," I told him, my eyes still closed. "I don't want a ring like Mom's anymore. I want an automatic foot rubba," I added, imitating his accent.

"We'll do that when you wake up. Try to go back to sleep. Okay, pumpkin pie?"

I nodded my head and took a deep breath, waiting for the medicine to work its magic and for Mom's bed to swallow me up in its sweet-smelling, soft embrace.

●　◆　●

Over the course of days, then weeks, I adjusted to the idea that the metal in my legs wasn't going anywhere—not until I was four inches taller. My musical tastes during this time changed, too, from my pop favorites like Cyndi and Debbie Gibson to hair bands and hard rock.

After school, Katie would often visit me and together we'd watch Bret Michaels and Guns N' Roses videos on MTV. We'd giggle and quickly flip the channels back and forth, timing it perfectly when Mom came and left the living room. MTV was forbidden in my house and I loved the chance to rebel, even a little bit.

I devoured every detail Katie divulged to me about school. Without her, my days consisted of homework from my tutor, range-of-motion exercises, stretching, and cleaning and turning my pins.

Turning the pins, despite its torturous terminology, was actually the easiest part about the entire lengthening process. Unlike the tools I'd created from household items when I was younger, I now used an official tool that Dr. Shapiro had given me right out of the hospital cabinet. It was called an L-wrench and I kept it by my side at all times, even though I only needed it to turn the pins four times a day. The wrench had become a part of me—or maybe part of the person I was going to be. Four times a day I'd stick the short end of the wrench into a hole of the apparatus and crank it counterclockwise. At eight in the morning, at noon, at six in the evening, and finally, at midnight, I'd stretch my bones for a total of one millimeter a day. And I didn't feel a thing.

Cleaning the pin sites was more tedious than turning them. Every night, just before bedtime, I dipped oversize Q-tips into hydrogen peroxide and swiped them along the sites where the pins entered my skin and went into the bone. I pressed and then dragged the skin away from each pin to prevent it from growing upward and becoming inflamed and infected.

But the most defining part of the whole bone-lengthening procedure was the exercising. I had absolutely no choice but to do it—if I didn't, my muscles would lock up and, as Mom explained it, the surgery wouldn't work. I wouldn't be able to gain the full two inches in my tibias. Everything was connected—my ligaments, my skin, my nerves—and they all needed to be stretched together to keep up with the stretching bone. Though I couldn't fully understand the medical explanation, I did understand that the more I stretched, the less the tremors wreaked havoc inside me and the easier I could sleep.

Exercising every day broke me down and then built me back up again. I learned how to control the pain instead of letting the pain control me. Together, Mom and I sat on the living room floor and I reached for my toes. The muscles in my calves clamped and the skin circling my pins pulled and burned as I reached forward. My stomach felt tight and hard as I tried to pull my toes toward my fingertips. I was only inches away from touching my feet, but in my world, inches felt like miles.

"Don't let it beat you," Mom ordered when another leg spasm crept up my leg as I stretched. "Breathe deep, in and out!" She wanted me to learn how to regulate my breathing. I learned another, more important lesson in those days as well: the more I controlled my pain, the less pain my dad experienced with my mom.

Throughout my lengthening process, I learned how to identify each hurtful sensation, and even to categorize it as being muscle, bone, nerve, or vascular pain. Muscle pain was sharp and stung rapidly. More often than not, vascular pain followed shortly thereafter. That was a throbbing sensation and it made my limbs feel cool or numb. Bone pain felt cold and penetrated deeper inside. The worst was nerve pain; it was a relentless mixture of all those sensations, and there was no rhyme or reason as to when it would strike.

Once in a while, I'd feel temporarily defeated, and, like clockwork, another argument would develop between my parents and the four-letter words would fly. It was my job to capture the pain and get it under control.

As I continued stretching, my eyes began to hurt from squeezing them shut and my vision blurred. My arms felt heavy as I stretched them forward. My teeth hurt from clenching my jaw and then my ears began to ring, but Mom kept coaching me.

"Don't lose control. Breathe! Take deep breaths, nice and slow," Mom shouted over my wailing.

From down in the basement, I could hear my dad vacuuming. The grinding of the vacuum motor was, I'm sure, his way of drowning out the crying and yelling.

This was my introduction—my training—to learning how to cope with true adult pain, and the harsh realities of diastrophic dysplasia.

"Don't let it win. Don't let the pain win. Toughen up. Fight!" Mom told me. "Count backwards from five and we'll be done," she promised.

"Five," I choked out between carefully timed breaths.

"Fight for *yourself*," Mom coached me.

"Four!"

"You'll never get anywhere in this world unless you fight. Remember this!"

I heard her loud and clear as I considered the vast difference between the way my mom handled problems and the way my dad ran from them.

"Three!"

"Fight to reach those doorknobs! Fight to reach Daddy's stereo! Fight to see above the dining table!"

"Two!" I wanted to help *set* the dining table. I wanted to see over the windowsill and reach every doorknob in the world so I'd never get stuck again.

"Fight to live your life, Tiffie."

I meant to shout the final number at the top of my lungs, but another word came out instead.

"*Fight!*"

After a month or two of turning my pins day after day, I gradually began to notice that the tiny difference in my legs was becoming a big one. I no longer needed pots or cookbooks to reach the things I desired.

I could see above the dining table and help set it, too.

My shoes were no longer easy to tie, as my feet stretched farther away from my reach. I could look down into my bedside table drawer and actually take in the mess that it had become. I could even reach the top of my dresser, and I could see, just barely, the top of my forehead in the mirror.

And for the first time, I felt the shape of a rounded doorknob in my hand, as opposed to the handles my father installed at my height. It was firm and solid. It felt so good. It was a whole new world for me, and I felt that I'd earned it.

Dad may have hated her for it, but my mother made the right decision with the lengthening surgery. Soon, another operation was scheduled to take the pins out of the tibias in my shins and drill a new set into the femurs in my thighs. Altogether it was about two years of surgeries, recovery periods, and exercising until the pins came out. Then, all that remained were tiny clear bandages called Steri-Strips taped across the holes in my skin to help them close. These were my first battle wounds, and my first real sense of what it was like to be more independent.

My legs felt like feathers once they were free from all the metal, but they were also weak, and I struggled to stand and walk. Light bed linens felt like heavy down blankets and I could barely move my legs underneath them at first. The stretching continued, but now Dad turned off the vacuum. And one day, he came home and gave me a boom box of my own—with a fancy dual cassette player and removable speakers so that I could play music while I kept up with my rehab.

"I'm sorry," Dad began. "The Fair didn't have one in pink." He placed a black boom box in front of me with a smile.

It was topped with an enormous pink bow.

# CHAPTER 5

# Too Small for Texas

At my mother's air force swearing-in ceremony in Sudbury, Massachusetts. We moved to San Antonio shortly thereafter.

In JANUARY 1991, the Gulf War played out like a movie on TV. I sat in my living room, transfixed by the live shots of soldiers and marines in camouflage crossing the desert with loaded rifles. Elsewhere on the dial, tanks fired and bombs exploded, and suddenly the idea of war—previously relegated to history books—felt very real.

One unseasonably warm winter afternoon, *he* was coming over: a recruiter from the US Air Force. Mom wanted to enlist. Not long before, she'd announced to my dad that she wanted to do her part for our country and work with the troops that we'd seen on TV.

"It's never too late to do what you want to do in life," I'd heard her say on many occasions.

Our front door was open, and the screen let in the breeze. I sat with my new, four-inch-longer legs stretched out in front of me, waiting. The Nintendo that Nick had let me borrow was plugged into our big, boxy TV, and I was excited to play his *Top Gun* game, which I'd specifically chosen for the recruiter's visit. It was my way of showing off.

With my fingers poised on the controller, ready to hit "start," I saw him. Dressed in a deep blue uniform with stripes and ribbons decorating his arms and chest, he was far more handsome than the camo-clad troops from TV. The recruiter's hair was dark and cut short, and when he smiled, he flashed a set of gorgeous white teeth that were as shiny as his black dress shoes. My mouth dropped open and my controller clattered to the floor. He was Superman. No, he was better than Superman, because Superman wasn't real, and this recruiter most certainly was.

As I stared at him, wondering whether he had flown in the jets I'd seen on commercials but feeling far too nervous to ask, he looked down at me through the screen.

"Hello," he said in a loud but friendly voice.

Mom then appeared from around the corner.

"Say hello, honey," she said as she welcomed him inside.

The recruiter walked in, removed his hat, and asked with a smile, "*Top Gun?*"

I stared at his uniform. There wasn't a wrinkle in sight. He was like a living, breathing billboard for the United States military, and all I could do was watch him in stunned silence, managing only a weak nod. It was one thing to see the jets and the bombs on TV and the men with rifles standing their ground without so much as a flinch. It was quite another to be in the presence of a man who may have actually sat under the dome of a fighter jet or behind the sights of a rifle.

"Outstanding," he replied, reaching into his bag and handing me a blue and white baseball cap. "Here," he said, handing it to me. "You'll need this."

The cap had a fighter jet stitched onto the front with red smoke trailing behind it. I watched my reflection grow larger in the recruiter's dark aviator sunglasses as he bent down to give me this fabulous gift.

While I got my bearings, the airman and my mom sat at our round dining room table, discussing all sorts of things I didn't understand and rustling papers between them. Mom looked back at me and smiled. I tried not to keep staring, but he looked so crisp, clean, and official. I couldn't understand how a person could look so handsome and so intimidating at the same time. Mom signed things, and he signed things, and throughout it all, no one asked my dad to sign anything.

"I have to do this, Gerry," I heard her say later that night. And then she issued an ultimatum of her own. "Come with us or we go on our own."

A couple of days later, Mom explained to me that we were going somewhere important where there were more men and women just like the recruiter, but that my dad had decided not to come with us. He didn't want to leave my brother.

I'd repeat part of my mom's reasoning in school when Katie asked me why we were moving. "We have to do this," I told her, even though I didn't understand why.

It was a confusing time for me, but I was used to feeling confused about my family—my dad's side, anyway. No one ever talked about the DiDonatos in front of me, but I did manage to hear bits and pieces about them from my parents' arguments. I never felt comfortable bringing up the subject myself.

I did think about the DiDonatos, but I didn't feel like a major piece of my life was missing without them, since I had no concept of who they were to begin with. I didn't even know if I had aunts, uncles, or cousins on my dad's side. No one ever said anything about my paternal grandparents, either. While I didn't spend time wishing for a reunion, I did wonder where they were and what they were like.

What sort of houses did they live in? Did I have cousins who were little like me? Did we shop at the same grocery store? Had I seen them there before without even knowing it?

During the holidays, I would only see my mom's side of the family. Every Thanksgiving, the Pryors would gather at Papa's long, wooden kitchen table to celebrate. My mom and dad took separate vehicles. Armed with their best side dishes, my family members would arrive, greeting one another loudly with hugs and kisses, and pats on the head for the kids. Then the group gathered in the den for hours to watch the football game before we sat down to eat. It was always a festive, happy mood around the dinner table.

But after the pumpkin pie was sliced and served, Dad would always leave early.

"It was good to see ya, Gerry," my aunts and uncles would say, the exact same way every year. Dad responded in kind. "Yah, yah, it was good to see you, too." Before long, it all started to sound very rehearsed to me.

"I'm just going to the store," Dad told me if I asked where he was going. Or, in his typical secretive fashion, sometimes he would simply say: "I'll see you back home."

Then he'd pull on his heavy brown coat, give me a hug without looking me in the eye, and shuffle down the narrow walkway from Papa's front door to the driveway. From the window, I'd watch him back his truck out onto the street and then I'd pretend, like my mom, that it was no big deal to go on with our holiday without him. But inside, I wondered where he went. Eventually I figured it out: Dad was going to see *his* side of the family.

And I wasn't allowed to go with him.

•◆•

Once Mom finalized her decision to enlist, she went away for special training. After what felt like a lifetime without her, Dad and I drove to Logan Airport in Boston. We looked up her gate on the big arrival screens, and I held his hand as we waited for her flight to arrive.

Mom was returning from MIMSO (Military Indoctrinated Medical Service Officer) training. As people filed off the plane and greeted their families, I spotted her. She was dressed in a deep blue skirt that touched just below her knees and a button-down blue dress shirt. Her hair was different. She had chopped off her gorgeous blond locks and returned with hair so short that it practically stuck to her head. Mom had a special pin on her shoulder and ribbons across her chest. She looked like one of *them*. I ran with my arms spread as wide as I could to hug her. I never wanted to be without her again.

•◆•

Our new home on the Medina air force base near San Antonio was sizzling, stifling, and flat. Mom and I were going to be stationed there for the next couple of years. The houses were made of brick or stucco and no one had wooden fences like so many back home in Douglas. Instead, tall stacks of gray cinder blocks outlined everyone's property and their windows were covered with twisted, wrought-iron bars that reminded me of black licorice. The whole neighborhood was outlined with barbed wire.

The houses weren't the only big differences from Massachusetts. Texas had snakes, fire ants, giant spiders, scorpions, torrential rainstorms, flash floods, tornadoes, and heat that didn't feel "dry" at all—someone had lied to us about that one. These new additions were poor replacements for the many things I missed dearly, like our stereo system, Bruiser, my Papa and his favorite dish that he would always make for me when I came to visit—linguine with clam sauce. And, of course, I missed my dad.

Mom and I moved into a plain-looking brick duplex fastened to a cement slab. The nameplate attached to the small parking pad read: *1st Lt. DiDonato.* That part always made me smile. In the background, rapid gunfire popped in the air. The airmen were doing training exercises, and I swore they were right in our backyard.

We walked into our new house through the kitchen door. Our moving truck took up the entire driveway and part of the street, too. Men wearing back supports hauled boxes upon boxes, each of them numbered with a neon orange tag, into our new home. While Mom stood with a clipboard in her hand, checking off each one, I took the opportunity to explore my new setting. I was disappointed to find that the kitchen was nothing special. It was cramped and stark white and it had just one tiny window above the sink—far too high for me to see out of it. The dining room was also small and opened up to the living room, which had a sliding glass door. I pressed my face up against the glass and peered out. We had the view of a dirt road, some stubby trees, and a big cactus. I wondered how many rattlesnakes might be curled up underneath.

"I can make anything look like home," Mom said, approaching me from behind. She rested a hand on my shoulder and gave me a kiss on the top of my head. I only came up to her waist.

"Everything is bigger in Texas," Mom had said on our last night in Douglas. "You'll love it!"

I wasn't so sure. Just when I had gained four inches, I was being whisked away to a place where things were even bigger than they were back home.

As I continued my tour of our new home, outfitted with a dull, cream-colored carpet throughout, I began feeling stuck between two places. I wanted to be with my mom while also wishing I were back home with Dad, and even my brother. But our house in Douglas had been rented out to strangers and Dad spent his days in the Webster apartment with Bruiser. I wanted our Bonneville back, too, because it was familiar and it was ours. But Mom had sold it and bought an electric blue Pontiac Grand Prix. There were colorful, glowing buttons splashed across the dashboard, and the car reminded me of a spaceship.

Texas may as well have been another planet.

In the living room, Mom plotted to fix the ugly carpet situation. She measured from corner to corner just before our couch and television were hauled inside. I squeezed past the movers, who barely seemed to notice me at all, and into my new room. I immediately zeroed in on the huge, floor-to-ceiling window. I'd have no problem gazing out on our sandy lawn. Things were looking up . . . until I noticed the closets. Two accordion-style doors were pulled open to reveal a single white wire shelf mounted high above my head.

How would I hang up my clothes? I thought frantically. How could I find Mom's cookbooks in all those boxes? Did we even remember to pack them? What if we hadn't?

Mom interrupted my panicked thoughts. "It will be easier to use this rather than looking for books and things to stack," she said, appearing in the doorway with a smile. I turned around to find her holding a grayish-blue Rubbermaid plastic stool.

I couldn't decide what I hated more: Mom thinking that I

couldn't help myself or the fact that I'd be forced to use yet another tool.

When the moving men finally pulled away from our new home, the sun began to set. I had hardly made a dent in unpacking my boxes, but I did manage to find my stuffed animals and Barbies. With the perfect sleeping companions selected, I began my climb up under the covers.

"Wait, no!" Mom shouted. "You can't just get into your bed here. Always check the sheets first."

"For *what*?" I asked.

"Anything," she replied, demonstrating how to carefully check every inch of the covers. I pictured all the creepy bugs that lived in Texas and shivered at the thought of them in bed with me.

Once Mom had determined that it was safe for me to squeeze between the sheets, she kissed me good night and switched off the light. I heard her walk toward the kitchen to continue unpacking and arranging all our stuff. I stayed awake for at least another hour, staring out into the hall and thinking about all the dangers and inconveniences in Texas: the insects, the closet, the heavy doors with rusted screens. And that was only in the house. I couldn't fathom what was waiting for me beyond our four walls.

The next morning in the bathroom, I was standing barefoot on my ugly blue stool to brush my teeth when something small and yellow caught my eye. It moved abruptly, raised its stinger over its body, and braced itself like it wanted to fight.

"Mom! Scorpion!"

She rushed in with her combat boot raised in the air, shouting, "I got it!" She swung the boot downward and it hit the vinyl floor with a hard *slap*, the laces whipping at the wall.

The crunch of the bug's skeleton made me cringe.

"I'll call Housing," she said calmly, scooping up the carcass with a spatula and flushing it down the toilet. "Don't forget to check your shoes before you put them on this morning," she added casually on her way out of the bathroom. "Things are a little different here."

"Don't forget to wash the spatula before you use it again!" I shouted after her. I heard her laugh from out in the living room. As I watched the remains of the scorpion swirl around the toilet bowl, I decided Mom was right: things were different here.

While we lived in Texas, Mom worked as a nurse at Wilford Hall Medical Center. On that first morning, we began what would become our routine: with her travel mug in hand and a backpack over my shoulders, we'd leave Medina, drive a few miles down the road, and then slowly roll through the gates of Lackland Air Force Base, where I went to middle school. Men armed with rifles and outfitted in head-to-toe camouflage stood at attention and saluted my mom when we drove through Lackland's gates. I always smiled and she did, too. It was so new, so exciting, and it made me feel like we might belong in Texas after all. We were important, or at least my mom was. Maybe what we were doing was important enough to leave our home up north, too.

"Want to see it again?" she asked with a laugh. I could feel how proud and happy she felt. It was a triumph for her in some way, and I wanted to share in her joy and in her moment.

"Yes!" I cheered.

With a sharp U-turn, we left base and reentered the front gates again. The sentry stood at attention and saluted once more without missing a beat. My mom's maneuver was a "butter bar" move (a slang term I'd learned for lieutenants who wore a single yellow bar on their lapels), but we felt we'd earned it. We had just uprooted our lives and left all that we knew, together. In a way, watching my mom get saluted made the day worth starting. It made us feel proud, bonded, and giddy, all at once. I wished my dad could see it and I wished I could have seen what my Papa looked like in his uniform when he served in the navy.

As we drove away from the gates toward my school, I watched a unit formation of airmen jogging across the sidewalks and through the grassy areas of the base. They chanted loud, rhyming cadences that kept everyone in step and their spirit stretched far beyond their group. I hung my head outside the open window, just to take it all in. There were decommissioned jets on display, monuments in the fields, and enormous American flags waving high above it all. I barely knew where to look first. I wanted to be a part of it all, to jog and chant even though I knew that my legs could never keep up.

My new school was as different as our new lifestyle. It wasn't even a regular building. I had to walk outdoors, on covered patios, to get to my math, English, and science classrooms, which my teachers called "portables." And when it rained, I had to struggle to use an umbrella that was bigger than I was. Worst of all, inside every classroom, waiting for me in a back corner of the room, was a Rubbermaid stool, identical to the one at home. They were following me.

"Your mom wants you to use this under your feet so your legs don't dangle," my teacher Mrs. Richardson said pleasantly. It was like peering up at a skyscraper to make eye contact with her. "It will help your circulation in your legs," she added, smiling.

Every day, I was reminded to place my stool under my feet. And every day I loathed doing it. The stool embarrassed me. When I set it on the floor and slid it under my desk, it made a hollow, clunking sound as if to remind the other kids—who seemed to be growing taller every week while I stayed the same size—that

I had to use it. I felt my cheeks grow hot each time someone swiveled around at his or her desk to look at me and my stool.

I could reach doorknobs now, but there was a host of new things that were out of my grasp, and just as many new things that I wanted to do. I wanted to see *over* countertops. I wanted to use the sink without dragging my stool into the bathroom with me. I wanted to sit in a chair like everyone else and use the chalkboard when the teacher called on me for answers.

More than anything, I wanted to be like Sarah.

Sarah lived across the street from me on Medina and she was in every one of my classes. Her mom consistently won the Garden of the Month prize on base and I was sure she used each fifty-dollar gift certificate that she was awarded on new clothes for Sarah. Every week, Sarah came to school in a new outfit: a matching, beautiful ensemble that complemented her colorful headbands.

My OshKosh B'gosh overalls weren't cutting it.

Sarah wore colored jeans and flip-flops, tank tops in the summer, sweaters and cardigans in the fall. Her short brown hair was so much neater and prettier than my messy ponytail that I couldn't reach to adjust. My arms were too short even to fix my own hair, I thought sadly as I gazed at her stick-straight locks while she ran her fingers through her perfectly cut bangs during English class.

I'd never seen clothes like hers when I went shopping, either—the stores where I got my wardrobe were geared toward small children, not preteens like me. I didn't know where Sarah shopped, but I knew the stores where my mom and I went did not have long jeans with the brand name stitched on the back pocket. Instead, I was stuck with the little girls' stores—those were the only sizes I could wear.

No one in my classes talked about my size or teased me about my clothes, but I couldn't ignore the difference between what I wore to school and what my classmates wore. And *that* made me feel different. It's funny how something as simple as a pair of jeans can make you feel normal. And I was certain these little things were what made Joshua Blackman notice Sarah.

Joshua and Sarah were an item, and they were the perfect fit. Joshua had blond hair, brown eyes, and a crooked smile. I was twelve and I had my very first crush. Each time he offered to sharpen my pencil for me because I couldn't reach the sharpener on my own—something I felt newly ashamed of—I found myself wishing I had what Sarah did. I wanted him to hold *my* hand and walk with *me* back to my desk like he did for her. Joshua was nice, he was funny, and he always raised his hand in Mrs. Richardson's class. But it didn't diminish his cool. He was the most popular boy in our middle school and he liked to eat lunch with a boy from Guam (a far-off, exotic place that instantly made him interesting).

I had two types of friends in middle school: those who liked to help me, carrying my things and looking out for me in the hallway so I wouldn't get trampled, and those who genuinely wanted to come over after school. Evelyn was the only friend I had in that second category. She had bright orange hair that barely touched the tips of her shoulders and she regularly pinned half of it up with a silver clip. She came over once a week after school and on the drive back to Medina, my mom, Evelyn, and I would stop at the USMC car wash.

In tight red T-shirts with gold bulldogs printed on their wet chests, the marines would be waiting for cars to scrub down with soapy water. They had a way of corralling even the cleanest of vehicles over to their corner in a parking lot. They chanted in unison and flexed their muscles. Every time, I swooned.

Their haircuts were higher and tighter than those on the airmen I was used to seeing around base. The marines spoke louder, stepped prouder, smiled wider, and looked tougher. I thought back to the war I watched unfold on TV and wondered how many of them went overseas. In person, they hardly seemed human. The marines who scrubbed Mom's car—the suds dripping off of every contour of their chiseled arms as we giggled inside—were not just handsome. They were perfection. Joshua should be a marine, I thought to myself at the car wash. He'd make a good one.

"One, two, three, four—Marine Corps! One, two, three, four— Marine Corps!" they chanted in unison. "The Army and Navy were not for me—Marine Corps! Air Force was just too easy— Marine Corps! What I need is a little bit more—Marine Corps! I need a life that is hard-core—Marine Corps!"

As we pulled away from the parking lot, I turned and stood on the backseat, peering out the rear windshield. "Hey! Air Force! Where're you going? Get in your planes and follow me!" Evelyn and I chanted. "I'm a United States Marine!"

One day at school, Evelyn told me that her dad had received orders to London. She was leaving in a month, and I was losing my best friend.

"I hate it here. I want to go home," I blurted out to my mom over dinner that night.

"Where is this coming from?" She had barely had time for a bite before I made my declaration.

"I just want to go home. I've always wanted to go back."

"We can't yet. We're here for a little while longer, okay?"

"No! It's not okay. When are we leaving? When are we done?" I demanded. "All my friends are leaving; why can't we?"

"What do you mean?"

"Evelyn is going to England. Her dad has orders to go there for four years." At twelve years old, that seemed like a lifetime.

"You're friendly, sweetheart. You'll make more friends, don't worry. You always do. And you can keep in touch with Evelyn, write letters and stuff."

"I don't want to make new friends!" I snapped. "I want to keep the friends I already have!"

"I understand that, Tiffanie, but . . ."

When Mom called me Tiffanie instead of Tiff or Tiffie, I knew that her patience was thinning, and I usually backed off of whatever I was whining about. But this time, I didn't care. I wanted to be heard.

"I hate it here and I want to go home. Now!" I shouted, slamming my hand down on the table for emphasis.

My mom was shocked—I'd never yelled at her before. But she still wasn't going to allow it.

"That's it! Get to your room right now!"

"No! I'm not in the air force; you can't give me orders, *ma'am*!"

"Excuse me, fresh mouth?"

It was the wrong button to push and I couldn't meet Mom's stare as she looked at me with her lips pursed together, eyes narrowed.

"I said: *Get to your room!*"

Fuming, I swallowed the angry lump in my throat, slid off my chair, and waddled down the narrow hallway that led to my bedroom. Before I slammed my door, I yelled back: "And I hate your hair!"

Refusing to use my blue plastic stool to get onto the bed, I clawed my way up, hot tears streaming down my cheeks by the time I threw myself into the pillow. A few minutes later there was a knock on my door.

"Tiffie?" Mom paused. "Tiffie, can I come in?"

I didn't answer.

Quietly, she pushed the door open. She moved my stuffed animals aside and sat next to me on the bed but didn't say a word. That's always been the beauty of my relationship with my mom. We could fight one moment and be perfectly normal the next.

"Why isn't Dad here?" I asked, sobbing.

"He has things in Massachusetts to take care of. You know that."

"Can I call him?" I asked.

"Of course you can call him." She got up and retrieved the phone for me.

"Daddy," I sobbed over the line, "I miss you. I want to come home."

A year or so later, I got what I wanted. Mom didn't reenlist for reasons I didn't fully understand. I still don't (she's incredibly private about it), though I suspect it had something to do with me. At the time, I was just happy we were leaving. But every time I hear my mother tell someone, "I'd give my right arm to go back in," I feel a little more guilty and responsible for it all.

Back home in Douglas, life was nothing like I'd hoped it would be. Everyone had moved on. Even though I grew up with those kids, when I returned, I felt like I didn't know them at all, and they didn't know me. They had shared memories and inside jokes I had no way of understanding. I wondered if Evelyn felt the same way at her new school in London. Luckily, I still had Katie, Bruiser, and my old closet with shelves that I could actually reach. But that was about to change. Again.

For my thirteenth birthday, I wanted nothing more than new clothes. So Dad took me out on a birthday shopping spree. Inside the massive expanse of Filene's department store, I was surrounded by more "Sarahs" who looked nothing like me. I thought back to my days with my dad at the Fair when nothing mattered but which Barbie I would pick. Now I had to look like the Sarahs of the world.

"Are you hungry?" Dad asked me after a couple of hours of sorting through tops and skirts and dresses. Shortly thereafter, we plopped down on plastic chairs in the food court.

"Dad, what makes a girl pretty?" I asked.

"I suppose it's different for everyone," he said thoughtfully.

"I don't think my hips are pretty—they're wide," I said between bites of sweet-and-sour chicken with fried rice.

"You ever see this expression?" Dad asked, forming the shape of an hourglass in the air with his hands. "There's nothing wrong with wide hips."

"I've never seen that," I told him.

"Oh. Well, don't worry about what someone else thinks is pretty. Worry about what makes you happy. Pretty will come through being happy."

This was the best piece of advice my dad had ever given me.

As we pulled into the driveway after our shopping trip, something on the front walkway caught my eye. As I made my way up to the front door, I was shocked to see that it was a For Sale sign. Through the screen door, I watched Mom talking to a man at our dining room table, both of them signing papers. The man wore cowboy boots that poked out from beneath his stonewashed jeans. I looked at my dad, who remained stoic as he watched them.

*Not Texas*, I thought wildly. *Not again!*

"Tiffie," Mom began as I walked into the house, "this is Randy Carpenter. He's our Realtor." Randy smiled and shook my hand.

"Are we leaving again?" I asked, feeling frantic.

"We're going to stay with Papa for a while in Marlborough."

As I stood there trying to process the shock of a move in

progress that no one had told me about—and one that Dad didn't seem to be involved in—Mom smiled at me.

"Did you have fun shopping, Miss Teenager?" she asked, as if nothing had just happened. "We have cake for you!"

Soon, our house in Douglas was sold—because, I learned, Mom wanted to live closer to Papa—and I felt uprooted all over again. Along with my friends, my sense of ease in the world had vanished. I hated struggling to put in my own earrings, barely able to reach my own ears. I hated not being able to reach the perfume bottles on my dresser or the forks in the drawer. I was too stubborn to ask for help, and the process of finagling clever tricks to function during my day didn't make me feel like MacGyver anymore. It was just frustrating. I was no longer in my house where I could find whatever I needed and make the space work for me. In Papa's house, I didn't feel right about rummaging through his things to find household items I could use as tools.

On nights while Mom worked, Papa and I often made our favorite meal together: linguine with white clam sauce. As we cooked, Sinatra and Dean Martin played softly, and we shook our hips to "New York, New York." While Papa moved about the kitchen, gathering ingredients, I dragged my stool around with me.

One night, like an hourglass that had run out of sand, time had run out on my patience. I woke up after midnight with a mean craving for Oreos and milk. Quietly, and careful not to wake my mom and Papa, I followed the glow of the night-light down the hall to the kitchen. The Oreos were close by on the shelf, and I could reach them easily. The milk would be more of a problem.

As softly as I could, I opened the refrigerator and placed my stool up against the shelves. The milk was on the fourth shelf. As I had done so many times before, I stepped up and felt the ribbed plastic underneath my bare feet. Closer and closer, I carefully moved my toes to the smooth edge and squeezed my butt for balance. The bright bulb felt hot on my eyes as I gazed up at the milk.

I stretched my tiny arms up as far as I could and stood on my tiptoes until I felt the plastic gallon container against my fingertips. I squeezed hard with both hands and pulled it closer, inch by inch. I lifted my body higher with my toes. I had it.

I almost had it.

I *would* have had it if I could have held the jug tightly with my hands, but its width and weight were too much for my small arms.

Then I lost my grip.

The milk jug somersaulted down to the floor and hit the tile with a thud. The lid popped off and bounced under the cabinets. I was too shocked to notice that my feet had begun to slip as well. Suddenly my stool shot out from under me and I went crashing down to the floor.

I landed hard on top of the jug and rolled over onto the cold milk still pouring out. I was drenched. The milk flowed around my head, soaking my nightgown and my hair. I lay there staring hard at the ceiling. The adrenaline coursed through my veins, and my nose tingled like I was about to cry. This was an accident that never should have happened. I wanted cookies and milk, but instead I got a harsh message, loud and clear. I was not finished with my bone-lengthening surgeries.

"What are you *doing?*" Mom yelled as she barreled down the stairs. Papa swung open the door from his bedroom and met her in the kitchen. I looked up at them from the floor but didn't answer. I was busy picturing Sarah reaching into her refrigerator and easily, effortlessly, pouring herself milk without falling and scaring her entire family.

"You're lucky that wasn't glass!" Papa boomed. "Did you hurt yourself?"

I didn't know how to answer. I wasn't physically hurt, but I was so frustrated by my own body. How could I start high school when I couldn't even get my own drink? What kind of teenager was I? What kind of woman would I be? Inside, I ached. I wanted to scream and slam my fists on the floor. I was angry with the fridge, angry at the milk, and angry at whoever had placed it on the fourth shelf. But above all, I was angry with my stubby arms. I stood up slowly with the help of my Papa's strong forearm and shot my mom a look that said it all.

I wanted longer arms and I didn't want to waste any time.

We were in Dr. Shapiro's office within days. "There's no use crying over spilled milk," he joked.

But it was more than that. I had been challenged, and I had lost. And any surgery that minimized the chances of that happening again would be well worth it.

"We could probably get two inches in your arms by lengthening the humerus," Dr. Shapiro said encouragingly. "You will be amazed at what two inches can give you."

Something told me he was right, and I decided that it would be well worth it to have the surgery on my arms.

## CHAPTER 6

# You're Obviously a Dwarf

As a teenager, with my mother and one of her patients
from UMass Memorial Medical Center (our Pontiac
Grand Prix is parked in the background).

MARLBOROUGH HIGH SCHOOL was a massive, three-story brick
building. It was imposing to everyone, but especially to me at an
even four feet tall. I attended eighth grade in the building due to
overcrowding in the middle school. Black panther paw prints
lined the outdoor walkway and two sets of double doors opened
into a large, open foyer at the front of the building. Bright orange
railings lined the stairs and second- and third-floor walkways, and
there were rumors that the design of the school was modeled after

a state penitentiary. I don't know how true this was, but I do
know that Mrs. Carlson, one of the headmasters, acted a lot like
a warden as she stood out in the first-floor hallway, ordering us
into our classrooms.

As in every high school, Marlborough had its cliques. Stepha-
nie, Jessica, Clarissa, and Kelly were the ambassadors of the "in"
crowd. I wanted terribly to belong, but since I didn't, I remember
taking pride in the fact that Mike Gould, the guy that all those
girls wanted, would call *me* after school each day.

Mike went to Northborough, a high school in the next town
over. All the girls flocked to him for as long as I can remember, no
matter what school they attended. They all loved him and wished
he'd love them back. He was the boy everyone wanted at their
party, because he *made* the party, just by entering the room. With
deep brown eyes, chestnut hair, and a perfect smile—accessorized
with a pair of round dimples—Mike was the portrait of what it's
like to be exceptional. If it weren't for his slight lisp, he probably
would have been *too* perfect, but on a guy like this, even a minor
speech impediment was cute. He knew all the popular people
from all the neighboring high schools: the Southborough ninth-
grade girls, Westborough's eleventh-grade babes, and the Hudson
twelfth-grade hotties. He dated them all briefly and left them pin-
ing. He was a legend and a bad boy who loved to ride dirt bikes,
and I had the luck to call him my best friend.

Every day after school, the phone would ring and I knew his
soft, sweet voice would be on the other end.

The greeting was always the same.

"Hey, what's up?"

And I always looked forward to telling him.

Our friendship started completely by accident, in the summer
of 1994, just after my mom and I moved out of Papa's house and

into a saltbox-style home of our own where Dad moved in with us for good. I was fourteen, I had never had a date or a boyfriend, and Mike was in the middle of an adolescent love triangle with my friends Jen and Megan.

"I'm done! He has to choose—it's me or Megan!" I remember Jen announcing dramatically one day at my house. She came over often and I'd get to hear about her latest saga. Jen was into cropped shirts, lip gloss, eyeliner, blue eye shadow, and boys who owned beepers. She was a nice, normal, and frivolous distraction from the seriousness of surgery I often faced. That afternoon, she reached for the phone and thrust it in my direction after dialing Mike's number, disregarding my mom's strict policy against calling boys.

"Find out how he feels about me," she ordered.

"He won't know who I am," I said softly.

This would be the first time I had ever spoken to a boy on the phone. Nothing compared to the nervousness I felt that day as I gripped our cordless phone—not needles, not hospitals, not operating tables. Mike and I had never actually met, but his reputation preceded him. I was scared.

"It doesn't matter," Jen reassured me. "Just tell him you're my friend."

So I did. The call was easier than I thought, and that night Mike picked neither Jen nor Megan to date. Instead he went out with Christine, a girl from the tortured, teenage-angsty crowd at my school. Within the next few days, Jen had found a new boy to obsess over. He even had a beeper. Megan, on the other hand, didn't get over Mike quite so quickly, and I happily lent her my ear for it.

A few days later, I got a surprise phone call. Mike called *me* to talk. It had been business as usual that afternoon, turning the pins in my forearms and cleaning them for the second time of the day, when the phone rang. (The fixator devices attached to my arms looked like long, horizontal remote controls—and the process was not nearly as painful as lengthening my legs.) I was shocked to find out that Mike was interested to know who I was and wanted to know why he'd never seen me before. It really bothered him. He knew everyone there was to know—how had little me escaped him?

"Who do you hang out with besides Jen? Where do you go to chill?" he asked me.

When I told him I hung out with doctors and nurses and actually spent a lot of my free time at the hospital, I guess I intrigued him because from that day forward, he never stopped calling. Our conversations lasted for hours. We talked about everything under the sun, just two people getting to know each other and enjoying the learning process.

"What movies do you like?" he asked.

"Comedies," I answered.

"Do you go to the Marlborough theater?"

"Not really," I said.

Other times our talks consisted of heavier topics, like the hidden meaning behind songs we heard on the radio and how, in our young and naive lives, it all seemed to relate to us. He strongly urged me to switch favorite musical genres.

"Boyz II Men?" he'd laugh, mockingly. "You need to hear Nirvana."

He did his best Kurt Cobain and sang a few lyrics of "Nevermind" over the phone with his guitar.

After a month of phone calls, that July I finally met the famous Mike face-to-face. My mom picked him up and brought him to our house. I waited anxiously under an umbrella at the patio table in the backyard for him to arrive. Katie stayed over that weekend to calm my nerves about meeting the boy I had been gabbing about. The night before, she and I had torn apart my closet for the perfect outfit I could feel comfortable in when I met Mike. Every pair of jeans I had purchased with my dad at Filene's were cut at the knees to fit my short legs. They frayed around my ankles and squared awkwardly over my sneakers, looking sloppy and unfinished. They were the only pants I had, other than the pastel pink leggings I had yet to throw out from Texas.

The afternoon of Mike's visit, I chose denim shorts and an oversized short-sleeved green T-shirt from UMass hospital. The sleeves easily covered the tops of my pins. It wasn't the most fashionable outfit, but it was comfortable, and it spoke to a part of my life not many understood—but that Mike promised to try to comprehend. He wore a baseball cap and long, baggy shorts and brought a friend named Mike Dufault, or "Dufe" for short.

Mike didn't even say hello when he came around back. Instead, he pulled out a Nirvana CD.

"Got a radio?" he asked. Then he sat down next to me, casually, as though we were lifelong friends.

We all sat and listened as the sounds of Cobain's mournful guitar filled the yard. When Mike noticed the pins in my arms, I was relieved to find out that he wasn't afraid or grossed out.

"Does it hurt?" he asked.

I told him it didn't.

"How long do they stay in again?" He stared at the pins, then back at me.

"Until I can reach the top of my head," I responded.

A few moments passed in silence.

"If a monster came in here right now with a gun, Dufe, would you run?" Mike asked randomly.

"No shit," Dufe quipped, and we all laughed.

Mike faced Katie and asked her the same question.

"Yeah!" she squealed.

"I wouldn't," Mike said. Then he turned to face me. "I'd stay here with you, because you can't run. I'd stay right here."

My heart raced and I looked away from his eyes, feeling a rush of excitement and shyness at the same time.

• ◆ •

That fall, the pins in my arms were removed and I became a high school freshman. Most days, I ate lunch with a girl named Kelly Joyce, who was easily one of the tallest girls in school at five foot ten. She always offered to get my lunch for me (I couldn't see over the buffet, let alone reach it) and in return, she'd get to snag an extra plate of fries for herself. Kids teased Kelly for her height and called her "Jurassic Joyce." You just can't win.

After an incident in junior high when I passed out from lugging my heavy book bag down two corridors, I was no longer allowed to carry my own belongings. I had needed to get from one end of the junior high school to another, and, as always, I would drag my green book bag by its straps. It was so heavy that wearing it on my shoulders would literally pull me over backward. But dragging it down the hallways was incredibly draining. By the time I got to my classroom, I just toppled over, like a turtle flipped over on its shell. That was the end of dragging my backpack.

Megan and I were still good friends and had nearly every class together. In high school, Megan volunteered to carry the extra weight. Together we walked to each class and she'd keep in step with my short gait, becoming something of a barrier between me and the other students who might not even *see* me walking.

During one of our hallway expeditions, she talked me into joining the Marlborough High sports medicine team.

Mike thought it was a great idea to get me out of my shell. Medical tape, injuries, bandages, bruising, strained muscles—I was familiar with them all. And this was an activity I could do with a friend, and a place where I could belong. I was looking forward to the memories before I even got started. I couldn't wait to wear—to *earn*—my team jacket.

The sports medicine room was small, making it crowded for the half dozen students who waited around inside. The coach's desk sat in the far corner of the room, and an ice machine rumbled next to it. Metal racks filled with supplies lined one orange-striped wall, while two wobbly padded beds and a small hot tub took up the remainder of the space.

After a considerable wait and excited whispering among my classmates, Ms. Hart stomped into the room. She had long, thick legs and wild hair that ran down her back. Hauling an armful of files with a stiff, cold expression, she didn't smile at any of us when she entered. But she did appear to size us up before she finally began speaking.

"First thing all of you need to learn is how to rip tape," she said through tight lips. No "hello," no "welcome to the club." Just instructions.

Everything was strictly business. It never occurred to me to find that odd or take it personally. I assumed that was just her way. "When you're out on the field, you'll need to bandage an athlete quickly, and the faster you can rip tape, the better," she said, picking up rolls of medical tape from the racks. "This is how you do it."

With her pointer finger and thumb pressed firmly on the edge of the tape, she tore off a piece in one swift movement.

"Understand?" she asked, fixing her gaze on me. She tore another piece of tape, and then slapped it on her thigh. She tore over and over again, shredding through the roll with ease.

"Go practice."

Megan and I grabbed some tape and stood by the two beds, where we decided to stick the torn pieces. For Megan, it was no problem tearing through the thick white roll. For me, it was a little harder. I could grip the roll, but pulling it and tearing with enough dexterity to quickly rip the tape was not happening. My little hands didn't have the strength.

"Come on, Tiff. I'm beating you," Megan joked, sticking her fifth piece of tape on the edge of the bed. She was only kidding, but I envied the ease with which she completed the activity. Not to mention the ease of just being her. Megan always wore her blond hair in a ponytail, pulled halfway through the elastic. Her bangs were neatly curled with a blow-dryer and round brush—the premier style of the mid-'90s. She wore easy-fitting clothes, like a T-shirt and jeans, paired with big, silver hoop earrings. Her style reflected her personality, and her big, confident smile made her inviting. Megan was not a girly girl. She was easygoing, fun, and athletic. I wished I could be more like her.

As I stood there trying to figure a way to catch up, something shiny caught my eye: a pair of medical scissors hanging on a little hook behind mountains of gauze.

"Oh, really?" I shot back to Megan, already confident that I'd found a way to win.

I grabbed the scissors with a smile and began to cut the tape as quickly as she tore. I'd watched nurses do this on many an occasion when I was in the hospital, so I knew what I was doing. And I did it well.

Soon Megan and I were even, and I felt like a pro. Like I belonged. Megan and I giggled our way through two rolls of tape, and in the midst of our race, I thought I noticed Ms. Hart scowling at me. I pressed on anyway.

Then we moved on to a new task.

"Not everything you deal with on the field will be easy," Ms. Hart said.

She narrowed her stare in my direction. I pretended not to notice.

"When there's an injury, we apply ice. Sometimes the ice feels worse than the injury, but our job is to make sure they keep it on their bodies. How can we tell them to do this if we don't know what it feels like? For five minutes you are all going to take turns placing your foot in this bucket."

She scooped ice out of the ice machine and into a small trash can while everyone looked at one another. *Is she serious?*

But Ms. Hart was not the type of teacher you defied. One by one, my fellow students took off a single shoe and sock and stepped into the bucket, grimacing and giggling as quietly as possible. I lined up last. Secretly, I was hoping the clock would wind down and we'd be done for the day, letting me quietly skip out on the assignment. It was not that I didn't want to do it. I would have *loved* to deal with the crazy, painful assignment just like everyone else, and to laugh and joke about how badly it sucked to sit there with my foot inside a bucket of ice. I wanted so much to be just like everyone else.

But I couldn't.

I knew that the amount of pain I'd feel in my muscles and joints would exceed the pain felt by anyone else. Thanks to all the surgeries I'd been through and the fact that my disability played on the same team as severe arthritis, the ice wouldn't just sting and then numb my foot. It would pierce my joints, creep up my leg, and take every muscle in my body hostage for the rest of the night. It would prevent me from moving my foot and leg, and from functioning for hours after I left school. Even if I sat down for the rest of the night, or just went to bed, I would still feel the chill of the ice controlling me. My arthritis would have a celebration in my body. I was no stranger to pain. I respected it, but the pain I endured was for a reason.

"Ms. Hart?" I began softly when it was my turn. I stepped toward her desk, motioning for her to come closer to me.

"Yes?"

"Can I speak to you for a moment?" I nodded toward the door, hoping to move her away from the other students.

"What is it?" she said. She wasn't budging.

"Is there something else I can do?" I said softly.

"What?" she replied loudly.

"Is there, um, maybe, something else I could do instead?" I repeated hopefully. "I've had a lot of surgery on my feet."

She stared at me blankly.

"I don't think it's a good idea for me to do . . ."

"You need to feel what the athletes will feel," she replied loudly.

"Yes, I know. But could I place my hand in the ice instead?" I suggested, showing her my scar-free extremity. "I'll still feel the cold and I'll still understand the athletes. I haven't had surgery on my hands, see?"

She stared back at me hard. It made me nervous. Her gaze was blank and uncaring.

Swiftly, she moved the bucket aside and placed two egg crates in the center of the room.

"Let's talk."

She sat on one, and then motioned for me to do the same. For a moment I thought she was preparing for me to do something else—maybe she'd be a mock patient. Perhaps she was going to pretend to be a difficult football player who needed to be bandaged with ice. Maybe this gruff teacher wanted to see how I would handle the situation, I thought excitedly, and I readied myself to impress her.

Nothing could have prepared me for what I heard her say next.

"Look, I don't know what kind of disease you have, but you're obviously a *dwarf*. Why don't you tell me what you can and cannot do?"

I suddenly felt sick to my stomach. Her words paralyzed me.

Ms. Hart inhaled deeply and continued.

"Maybe sports medicine isn't the best thing for you to do. Maybe you should find another activity."

Each word out of her mouth was sharp and jagged, puncturing my pride. Yet I was too frozen to respond.

I felt a wave of heat pass through me. I had never been told that I couldn't do something. It went against everything I was raised to believe. What was she talking about, a disease? And a dwarf? I knew I was born with a bone condition, but a dwarf? And I had a *disease* on top of that? Why hadn't my parents told me?

My eyes burned from holding back tears. I wanted to assault her with *my* words, hurting her back, but my breath was taken away. I couldn't move off that egg crate. I felt like I had met a monster. And Mike was right; I couldn't run away.

I could tell everyone else in the room had heard what she said, Megan included. But they all kept busy, avoiding my gaze as they bandaged already-wrapped ankles, and ripped tape until their rolls were empty. They were trying not to be there, and to act as though they hadn't noticed my humiliation. I felt so alone.

*Tell her she's wrong!* a little voice howled inside me. *Tell her you can do anything! Tiffanie, say* something!

I said nothing.

Instead, I stood up, and everyone looked away as I walked toward my backpack and then the door. Behind me, I heard Ms. Hart putting the egg crates back on the shelf. She had already gone back to business as usual.

I was so angry with myself for allowing everyone in the room to hear what she said to me, and for being too stunned to respond in any way.

When Mike called me that afternoon, I told him everything through tears and heaving sobs. Somehow I had managed to put on a fake smile for my mom as she drove me home, but as soon as I got on the phone with my friend, it all came out. I cried and cried and told him everything. Mike listened, quietly, until I was done. Then he had just one request. And despite my hesitation and embarrassment, I made my way downstairs to hand off the phone.

"Mom? Mike wants to talk to you."

●  ◆  ●

Like an angry tidal wave, my mother crashed into Marlborough High School the next morning. Mike had told her everything that I was too embarrassed to share. Her hands clenched into fists by her hips, my mom demanded to speak to the principal, Mr. Clemens; the vice principals, Mr. Clancy and Mrs. Carlson; and the head of the athletic department, Mr. Long. She did not, however, want Ms. Hart anywhere near her.

My father accompanied her on her quest for justice. I was along for the ride, too, even though I still felt more awkward and upset than vengeful. Once everyone was ready to meet, we all piled into a conference room. As far as I was concerned, I was simply going to retell what had happened and how it made me feel.

When we were all seated, Mr. Long shifted uncomfortably in his chair as he stared at the floor. He refused to raise his eyes to me as I spoke, or to make eye contact with my parents. He remained quiet and almost seemed threatened. But one of the vice principals looked right at me and asked a question that left me feeling sick to my stomach.

"Ms. Hart has been here for a while," she began. "Do you think it's possible that you misunderstood her?"

"Excuse me?" my mother barked before I could respond. "How can she *misunderstand* something that has never been said to her before?"

My dad didn't say a word at the conference table. His hands did the talking as they shook. Gritting his teeth, he picked at his cuticles and then at a paperclip, unfolding it with red, raw fingers. For a man who lives to fix things, this was the first time I could remember him really wanting to break something.

"Maybe we should bring Ms. Hart in here, so we can understand her side," Mr. Clemens suggested.

"*Her* side?" my mom snarled. "You bring that woman in here, and I can't promise she'll walk out."

That shut everyone up, and the three administrators sat still, unsure of their next moves. But I knew mine.

The people I was told to trust and go to when someone hurts you had pretty much turned their backs on me. They were unwilling to make the right moves to rectify the situation. The heaviness I felt in the sports medicine room began to fall around me again. I could feel it closing in. I was done with their meeting. I was done being blamed.

"Can I go to class?"

After a long pause, my dad spoke up.

"You want to go to class? Go ahead."

The grown-ups across from me, too afraid to face the issue, forced fake smiles as I slid off my seat. Everyone waited until I was out of the room before the verbal sparring resumed. Once in the hallway, I paused and covered my mouth with my hand. I knew the tears were coming but I didn't want anyone to hear me cry. I felt like I had been called not only a diseased dwarf but also a liar.

I couldn't fight for myself. And that made me feel even worse.

I wasn't really going to class—I just wanted to get out of that room. I walked as fast as my legs could carry me down the cinder-block hallways. I walked away from the skinny gray lockers and the class I was supposed to join. I walked until my vision became clouded with tears and I found myself alone in the girls' bathroom.

Again.

No one was inside. Aside from the sound of a dripping faucet and my heavy breathing, everything was calm and quiet. I entered a stall, locked the door, and slid to the ground, my heart thudding angrily. It felt like Ms. Hart had grabbed me by the back of the neck, forced me to my knees, and pushed me to stare at myself in a fun-house mirror. She made me look at myself in a way that I had never considered.

Did others always see me this way? Why had they kept it from me? Did the whole school know what had happened in the sports medicine room? The questions drove me mad. My stomach churned, my body felt like it was on fire, and all the blood drained out of my face as I lurched toward the toilet bowl to vomit.

I heaved until I had nothing left in me. Then I made my way over to the sink to wash my hands. Out of habit, I used the handicapped sink. Yet another way that I was different from everyone else, I thought, marveling at the fact that this had never really made an impression on me before. I didn't even think about it previously, just like average-size people probably don't think about which sink they use. Just as with my pair of tongs, my bathroom habits weren't something I thought a lot about. I glanced back at the stall marked with a handicapped sign, the toilet paper holder that was screwed to the wall lower than the rest, the lowered lock on the stall door, and even the damn soap dispenser. Everything was different, adjusted for *handicapped* people. Like me.

My stomach began to burn again with anger. And in that moment by the sink, I promised myself I would never, ever be told I could not do something because of my handicap. This would be the *last* time I would be singled out, excluded, pushed aside, or deemed unable to participate in something I wanted to do. I was ready to adapt—clearly, the world wasn't going to do that for me. I was ready to do what it took to get the life that I wanted. I was ready to fight and go to war against dwarfism. More surgery would be the only way.

That night, over dinner, I told my mom what I'd decided. "I want to go through it again," I said simply. Everyone in my house knew what "it" was. And she agreed. My dad was against it and he reacted as he did with anything that upset him to the core. He just walked away, acting like it was only a fleeting idea that would run its course. My mom and I were instantly on the same page, ready, together, to embark on the bone-lengthening path once again.

But this time there was one major difference. I wasn't going to settle for the conventional amount of growth. This time I was going to make the pain worth it. The problem would be finding a surgeon who would do the procedure on *my* terms.

## CHAPTER 7

# No Limits

One of the "before" shots Mom insisted
on taking the morning of my
bone-lengthening surgery.

"IF I ONLY wanted three inches, I'd go buy a pair of platform
shoes," I told Dr. Shapiro, my voice sounding more emotional
than I'd intended. My mom and I had scheduled a meeting with
him about undergoing more lengthening surgeries, and I'd been
looking forward to it for weeks. But my conservative surgeon
wasn't budging.

I sighed and looked around the room, plotting my next move.
The conversation felt like a chess game. Children's Hospital Boston was under renovation, and it hardly looked like the same
place from my childhood. I had bigger plans now.

My efforts to persuade Dr. Shapiro for more than those mea-
sly three inches were going nowhere, and I was frustrated. He had

been my orthopedic surgeon for all my life. I had grown to love him and trust him, but today, he was becoming just another obstacle. Not unlike a parent concerned for his child, Dr. Shapiro was fixated on the complications that could occur. He droned on and on about nerve injuries, delay in or failure of bone regeneration, muscle contractions, and premature bone consolidation. These were real concerns, of course: the hope in bone-lengthening surgery—not the guarantee, as I was often reminded—is that after the bone is broken and stretched apart, the body will fill in the gap. But I'd heard this about a million times before. After a while, his words began to fade and run together. His mouth was still moving, but it was like Charlie Brown's teacher talking in the cartoon, and all I could hear was unintelligible, garbled noise. I was so fixated on the liberating possibilities that I was more than willing to gamble for what I wanted.

Back then, bone-lengthening surgery was still considered to be radical. Not many doctors knew about it in the mid-'90s, and if they did, they didn't want to perform it since the procedure had not been perfected.

I couldn't care less. Dr. Shapiro agreed to perform another round of lengthening on me, but he was very clear that he would not go beyond the recommended three inches. It was that or nothing. For me, going through so much pain again for that little wasn't worth it. He left me with no choice. Mom and I said good-bye.

The next day, after eight hours of school and homework, she and I sat down at the kitchen table to have a snack together and discuss other doctors who might be able to perform the surgery the way I wanted it. There was Dr. Paley in Baltimore, whom we'd met with when I was little, but since he hadn't been the right fit for the first round of lengthening, we knew we had to look further.

"I was talking to Linda Johnson the other day during lunch," Mom said over our string cheese and apple slices. Linda was her friend at UMass who was also a pediatric nurse. "She asked me how you were doing and if we were still going forward with lengthening."

"What did you say?" I asked eagerly.

"I told her we were looking for a new doctor. She said we have a new surgeon at UMass, a Dr. Mortimer, and he does lengthening. He's from Montreal. Want me to make an appointment?"

I dropped my snack and stretched my arms out toward her.

"Yes!"

A couple of weeks later, Mom and I hit the road in her Jeep Cherokee, taking in a pink-hued sky as the sun began its slow nightly descent. As we coasted down the Massachusetts highway, with inexplicably little traffic, toward the UMass Medical Center, I felt like it was perfect timing for a new beginning. In my mind, we were literally driving toward my future.

The meeting with Dr. Mortimer meant so much, and it would determine even more. If it went well, I'd be that much closer to the sheer freedom of driving without leg extensions wired into my dream car. To shopping in clothing stores that weren't geared toward little girls, to throwing away my short, frayed jeans, and to ditching that damn stool.

"What are you thinking?" Mom asked as she drove. Her hands were steady and calm on the wheel despite the seriousness of the meeting awaiting us. She glanced over at me, waiting for my response, but I didn't know how to answer. My heart was racing as I daydreamed about what could be my new reality.

I glanced down at my feet, jutting out just barely beyond the edge of the seat in our Jeep. Closing my eyes, I imagined the pressure under my ankles from the edge of the car seat disappearing.

I envisioned my knees stretching over the seat edge, feeling the weight of my feet as they dangled below me.

"Nothing much," I told her.

By the time we were seated outside his office, the wait had become unbearable. All sorts of scenarios danced around in my head as I imagined our meeting. What if he said no like Dr. Shapiro? I couldn't think of any other options. Then again, he could say yes. . . .

"Nervous?" Mom asked.

"Anxious," I replied. I fidgeted and shifted in my chair as she perused the pamphlets on the wall. The hard plastic edge of the seat dug harder under my ankles and created a throb that matched the growing beat at my temples.

"I just want a yes or a no, know what I mean?"

"Don't give him a reason to say no," Mom replied. "Be confident and be yourself. You've been through it before. You know what it's like and what's to be expected."

"That wasn't enough with Dr. Shapiro."

"And if it's not enough with Dr. Mortimer, we keep looking," Mom said and then paused. "Don't have a defeatist attitude."

"What's 'defeatist' mean?"

"It means you're defeated before you even begin. How bad do you want this?"

My gaze wandered down the hall. A few seats away from me, a mother held her baby girl with a smile, nuzzling the baby's rosy cheeks with her nose and kissing her tiny forehead. A large diamond ring on her left hand caught my eye as she turned to her older child, a boy of about eight who had a long cast on his leg. It was decorated from toe to thigh with friends' signatures and funny drawings, and the boy and his mom were giggling together. I imagined he was there to get his cast removed. Maybe he broke his leg while playing sports.

"Bad," I whispered just loud enough for my mom to hear me. "I want this *bad*."

"Good. Remember what your Papa says: 'All or nothing.'"

I looked away from the family down the hall and repeated my mother's words.

"All or nothing."

Fight was in the Pryor blood. I always tried to make that family characteristic my own.

Then he emerged. I was finally getting a look at Dr. Mortimer.

I was instantly struck by how *young* he looked—far too young for all the experience my mom and I had heard about. His face was smooth—I couldn't detect a single wrinkle—and he smiled with a slightly rebellious air about him. With his curly, reddish hair and slim frame, he looked like a Canadian Doogie Howser, I thought to myself, stifling a smile. He looked *nothing* like what I'd expected. It was almost as if he could hardly believe he was an acclaimed surgeon himself, because he didn't wear the usual white coat, or even a conventional suit and tie. Instead, he wore a plain button-down shirt and insisted that I call him by his first name, Errol.

It was going to be a good meeting.

His office was different from the others I'd seen. There weren't certificates and awards hung neatly on the walls. It was messy and jumbled and I was practically climbing his cluttered walls with impatience. I needed an answer to my question: would he operate on me?

Errol began by talking about his work and his philosophy about bone-lengthening surgery. He spoke simply and didn't intimidate me with the big words and medical jargon I had come to expect. I sat in the center of the room in a wheelchair provided by the hospital since walking the halls was too much for my small stride. I kept switching my position from upright and attentive to slouched and antsy. Errol sat on a chair in front of me and never asked me why I wanted to have surgery. He never asked me to consider my decision a bit longer and then get back in touch with him. Instead he simply asked, "How are you doing?"

As soon as he finished his question I was off and running on a tangent of my own. When it was my turn to speak, I made my timeline clear: I wanted to get the procedure over as quickly and as effectively as possible. I wanted to graduate with my class, and I wanted to walk across the stage to get my diploma.

When his facial expression changed from soft and congenial to stern and stiffened, I gripped my seat and feared the worst.

"Do you understand the complications that can result from this surgery?" he asked somberly, looking me right in the eye.

"Yes," I answered honestly.

He leaned back a bit in his chair, seemingly relieved. "They should be expected. The problems that we can fix, we'll fix, without a doubt. It's the problems that we *can't* fix we want to really consider before going forward. The more we anticipate, the more of an upper hand we'll have."

Errol spoke as if he were drafting some sort of battle plan, as if already he had *agreed* to do the surgery, at least in his mind. Then the moment of truth arrived.

"How much length were you thinking?"

I smiled. "How much do you want to give me?"

Errol's eyebrows scrunched together, and suddenly I was nervous again. Perhaps I went a little too smart-ass with my answer.

"Well," he said, carefully measuring his words, "the apparatus is usually set in increments, and then it locks once it reaches the limit that we place on it."

"What if we didn't put a limit on it?" I asked, saying a silent prayer that he wouldn't dismiss me from his office right then and there.

Errol's eyes widened a bit.

"I want to determine my own limits," I continued.

"You know, gaining three or four inches is better than good; it's wonderful."

"Yeah, four inches is great, but it's not what I want."

"What exactly do you want?"

I paused, trying to figure out a way to make him understand. Errol sat back patiently, his eyes still locked on me. That was what I loved about him—he let me speak, and he treated me like an adult. I knew I had to tell him what I wanted without acting like an emotional child.

"Do you know what four inches feels like?" I asked. I wanted him to know I was a veteran and not going into all of this blindly.

He shook his head no.

"Four inches was more pain than I ever thought possible the first time I had surgery. Every night, I felt the muscles in my legs twitch and jolt and bang against me from the inside out. It was horrible, and while I was doing it, I swore I never wanted to feel that much pain again. But now I know that I *need* to do this again. I also need it to be worth all that pain."

There was silence. I don't think he or my mom had expected my response. I didn't really expect it, either.

"All right, I'll make you a deal," he said.

My attention was undivided.

"I'm going to need your help," he continued, shooting a glance at my mom. She nodded, inviting him to continue.

"I won't put a limit on the apparatus," he began, and my eyes immediately began to well up with tears. "But Tiffanie, I have to trust you here. You have to work with me. We have to work together on this. The more we stretch, the more pain you will experience and the more you run the risk of all those complications you hate hearing about. I need you to tell me when you can't take it anymore. I need you to promise to be honest with yourself, with your body, and with me. Can you *promise* that?"

"I promise," I said quickly, my voice cracking with joy.

"Even if your personal limit is only another four inches, will you *still* tell me you have had enough?"

"I will."

"Two inches?"

I paused. Two inches? What a horrible, cruel joke! He was crazy. Not while I'm in control, I thought. No way in hell would I accept only two inches!

"I promise."

He smiled and reached for my hand. "Deal."

I stared at his hand for a moment. This was it? We just made the deal? I looked at Errol, who was smiling. I realized I'd been holding my breath. I exhaled and smiled, too. It was just us, and we had come to an agreement. It felt so grown-up. I shook his hand and thanked him, ecstatic to be one step closer to my goal. I cried silently, feeling the tears roll down my cheeks as my mom, who had been silent thus far, let herself cry, too, as she shook Errol's hand.

From there, we talked specifics of the surgery. It would be similar to the one I had undergone as a child, with the pins drilled into my broken bones. Again, I'd turn the pins a quarter millimeter, four times a day, for a total of about an inch in added height per month. Because of the amount of height I wanted this time around, Errol would use a different technique called the Ilizarov method, in which multiple wires would be strung through the bones in my feet, around my tibias and fibulas, and then connect to the metal halos that would encircle my legs. The wires would act like bobby pins, holding the small bones in place. A thick, heavy nail would also be drilled through each of my heels.

I almost called off the surgery right then and there, I was so freaked out by the way Errol described it. But because I didn't want to place a limit on how far I could lengthen, he said it was necessary to use this new method. It would be like an internal cast, keeping my bones immobile as my shins grew longer, minimizing the chance for complications by allowing him to make tiny adjustments to keep my bones in proper alignment.

The nails in the heels sounded the worst to me. With them, I wouldn't be able to flex my feet or point my toes while enduring the lengthening. I could wiggle my toes, but the internal wires and nails would keep my feet flat. Somehow I was able to convince myself that it was just another part of the process, and though I hadn't experienced it before, I'd get through it just fine.

I'd simply come too far to turn back now.

October 15, 1996, was my last day at Marlborough High School. It was just like any other day. There was no big fuss signifying my farewell, no announcements, no homemade cupcakes to send me off. It was a little disappointing but not surprising: I didn't exactly make it public knowledge that I was undergoing major surgery to be followed by months of grueling recovery. Even if I had tried to explain it, I'm not sure my classmates would have fully grasped the concept.

When the bell rang at the end of my last day of school, the halls flooded with all sorts of bodies—thin cheerleaders, stocky athletes, scrawny sophomores, and heavy seniors (all of them tall, though), and they were all equally anxious to get the hell out for the day. Not me. I stood in the center of the atrium and I looked up at the bright orange railing lining the main stairway and the walkways to the left and right. Someday, I imagined, I would walk up those stairs, purposefully forgoing the handicapped elevator that I had relied on each day before. Taking the stairs with everyone else was a luxury I never got to experience. Someday, I promised myself as I gazed at the seniors upstairs, digging into their purses for car keys, I would drive my car to the school for a visit, and then effortlessly pull into a parking space of my own. One day, I would push open the front doors with ease, just like everyone else who passed by me on their way home.

I knew my mom was waiting outside in the parking lot, but I wanted to take my time saying good-bye. Other than Mike, I didn't tell anyone the extent of what was going to happen to me. The surgery would speak for itself. A few friends gathered around me and wished me good luck. Some said they'd write; others promised to visit. I smiled and nodded, encouraging their efforts but knowing that I wouldn't have any social life to speak of over the next several months.

But at least I'd have Mike.

I spent the majority of that evening compiling a mix tape for my Walkman. Bush, Republica, White Zombie, and random songs from the *Mortal Kombat* sound track made up what I would label "Surgery Mix." Mike had called me four times. The first two phone calls were extremely brief.

"Hey, what's up?" he began, as always.

"Making a mix tape," I said.

He didn't give me enough time to tell him I was including his favorite, Nirvana, before he got angry and hung up on me. I'd told Mike months earlier that I'd be undergoing more lengthening surgery, but he was dismissive of the idea from the start, saying I was fine just the way I was.

A half hour later he called back. He asked the same question and I responded the same way. He hung up. The third phone call lasted a bit longer.

"You're doing this all because of a teacher," he said.

"No, I'm not," I corrected him. "I'm doing this for me."

He hung up once more. Later that evening, he called to say good night.

"It's not too late to change your mind. No one is pushing you."

He was right, it wasn't one person pushing me, it was everything. My own *life* pushed me. I could tell he wasn't happy with my choice. Like my dad, Mike never understood how differently I saw myself. He could never comprehend just how hard it was for me to reach the milk off the top shelf in the refrigerator. To be eye to eye with Bruiser and to come up only to my friends' hips—I hated it all.

"I'm doing it."

"Fine."

"Call me in the morning to wake me up?"

"What time?" he asked with a dramatic sigh.

"Three a.m."

"Maybe."

And that was that.

The night before the operation was pretty unremarkable. We didn't have a big dinner. Despite the constant reminders from my mom to "eat what you want now, because at midnight, that's it," I wasn't very hungry.

I didn't even have any packing to do. What would I need? I wouldn't be able to wear socks or underwear. I didn't even need a toothbrush—the hospital provided one. I just needed my Walkman. Mom had the most to put together, because she would be staying the night with me. We watched television while she packed, and when it finally came time to turn out the lights, we said good night the same way we always did.

At three a.m. my phone didn't ring. I didn't sleep much and really didn't need a wake-up call, but I wanted to feel like Mike was there for me. My heart ached. I didn't want him to hate my decision, but I wasn't about to do anything to change it.

My dad was the first one up, making coffee. Mom took a brief shower and then carefully arranged my hair into a French braid— the best style for hair that would be pressed against a pillow, untouched for days. No one spoke much. It felt like we were all too busy going through our individual what-ifs. I pulled on my gray sweatpants and sweatshirt, gathered my headphones, and popped in my mix tape.

Once I'd made my way downstairs (the last time I'd have to do it like a child, sliding down on my butt, I thought to myself during the long trip down), my mom asked me to stand in front of the kitchen counter for pictures. I was annoyed. I didn't understand why she wanted them, since, to me, it didn't matter how I looked before the surgery. I just wanted the "after" so desperately that it angered me to see her holding up the process, even by a matter of minutes.

I complied with her request anyway. I tried to arrange my face into a neutral expression, but inside I was seething. My best friend in the entire world had failed to call me when I needed him most, and on top of that, I was asked to pose like a criminal for mug shots. I faced front, left, and then right, next to the counter. Then the phone rang.

I smiled with relief the moment I heard his voice, even if I didn't love the sentiment.

"This is your wake-up call . . . I think what you're doing is dumb," Mike said, his voice trailing off. "Are you scared?"

"A little."

"Here. Listen to this." The phone rustled a bit and then I heard him begin to strum his guitar to the tune of Bush's "Glycerine."

*I don't want this, remember that I'll never forget where you're at. Don't let the days go by . . .*

Mom motioned for me that it was time to go and I watched the clock on the stove tick from 3:29 to 3:30 a.m. Pre-op began at 4:00.

"Thanks," I told Mike. "Well, it's . . . about that time."

He took a short, shallow breath. "I'll say this for the last time, babes: You don't need this surgery. I love ya no matter which way you are."

I loved him for saying that, but my mind was made up. And I knew that he knew it, too.

"Have your mom call me afterward."

"Okay," I promised, so glad that he'd called after all. "I'll talk to you when it's over."

"Talk to you when it's over."

Outside, the garage door was open and the light illuminated the top of our driveway. I stood in front of the Jeep and looked one last time at my wobbly reflection in its cherry paint. I couldn't reach the door handle. Dad leaned over and opened it for me. I looked up at him and smiled, not because I was happy he did it for me, but because I wanted him to know I was happy to get in the car and go to the hospital.

"I'll be there a little later," he said. He was working a half day and would meet my mother at the hospital when his shift was over. I think he needed something to do during the surgery or else he'd be consumed with worry.

"Okay," I replied. And then we were off. It was that simple, that ordinary.

Mom wanted to talk, but I didn't have much to say. I just wanted to get the operation over with and move on to lengthening my legs. I felt impatient for the possibilities, and even more excited and ready to go, because it was finally all within my reach.

"What are you thinking?" Mom asked as she drove. Her hands were steady and calm on the wheel as always, despite the major surgery that was finally upon us. She occasionally glanced over in my direction, waiting for my response.

I didn't know how to answer her question honestly. Should I tell her what she wanted to hear? Did I tell her that I was confident, unafraid; that I'd undoubtedly made the right choice?

In actuality, I was thinking about those jeans again, childlike in their short length, and how much I couldn't wait to burn them. *I am making the decision to adapt*, I reminded myself. *The world will not.*

"I can turn around," Mom said gently, mistaking my silence for fear or regret.

"No!" I jolted out of my daydream. "Keep going. This is what I want."

"Do you mind if I stop for a coffee?" she asked.

"I don't mind."

"You sure? I always hate drinking my coffee in front of you when you can't have anything for yourself."

"I don't even like coffee," I reminded her. "Please, get some. It's fine."

A brief drive-through visit to purchase an extra-large coffee with three sugars and milk and we were back on the highway, merging onto Lincoln Street and then pulling into a parking space at UMass Memorial Medical Center.

In the pre-op room, the boxy TVs attached to the ceiling were set to the early morning news broadcasts. A team of doctors and nurses entered through the automatic room doors and a *swoosh* followed behind them as the doors shut tightly. The heavy scent of bleach floated toward me.

The residents stopped at the foot of my bed. Some kept their surgical masks pulled over their faces, while others appeared less intimidating and let their masks hang beneath their chins. They all checked my charts, flipping through the pages. The sound made me nervous. One nurse carried a gray plastic basket. She smiled and then walked closer. Inside were needles of all shapes and sizes, alcohol swabs, and other items for starting an IV. That time had come. I winced as she tied the yellow rubber band around my extended arm.

"Just relax," she said softly.

I hated this part.

I took a deep breath and exhaled and tried to ease my veins to the surface. If you're tense, I'd learned, veins dive like submarines. She tapped the top of my hand, trying to raise them back up to the surface. Then there was a pinch and an odd rolling feeling beneath my skin as my veins tried to move away from the blue butterfly 22-gauge needle. After a few more seconds, she was done. She flushed the line and then was on her way out of the pre-op room. Then my anesthesiologist finally approached.

My mom double-checked with him that the machine they used was halothane-free since I was allergic. Then he turned to me.

"Ready?" he asked.

More than ever, I thought as I nodded.

He inserted a needle loaded with the relaxant Versed into my IV's heparin lock and let me push it through at my own pace. I needed that sense of control and he graciously gave me that illusion. I turned up the volume of my headphones a bit, pushed the syringe forward carefully, and let my body ride the high. I felt weightless and giddy. Mom squeezed my hand and mouthed *I love you* as I got lost in the noise blaring from my headphones.

Then, casually, Errol entered.

I moved my headphones partially off my ears. The way Errol raised and then gripped the steel rails attached to my bed seemed slow and relaxed. Then he smiled and asked the same question as the first day I met him.

"How are you doing?"

"Errol," I responded as the Versed thickened my tongue, "I love you. I love you and I thank you. Thank you. I love you."

"I love you, too, Tiff," he replied as the fluorescent lights rolled by over my head. He placed his hand on my shoulder and walked beside my bed as the nurses wheeled me into the operating room. The massive, alienlike lights that hovered over the operating table made the room extremely bright. Someone close to me said, "Count to ten, Tiffanie," and out of the corner of my eye I watched the thick, milky propofol push slowly through my IV.

I made it to three.

# CHAPTER 8

# Learning to Walk Again

Sitting on the couch with the pins
and fixators attached to my legs.

It WAS DURING the evening that Mom realized she'd lost track of time. The hours seemed to meld together as she paced and made small talk with friends at the hospital while she waited for Errol to find her. A few times, she dialed the number the operating room nurse had given her to inquire about how I was doing. At other times, she flipped through the channels on the waiting room television, scanning everything but watching nothing. Mom never once left the hospital. The wait was approaching twelve hours and she grew more worried by the minute.

Soon, she calculated that thirteen hours had passed.

Then fourteen.

Finally Errol stepped off the elevator. Soaked with sweat as if he'd just stepped out of the shower, he hugged her and said the words she had waited all day to hear: "Tiffanie's done and she's doing fine."

It was the longest surgery I had ever endured.

"It took a while to erect everything around her legs, because her limbs are so short," he continued. "But she's doing fine." Beads of sweat continued to pour down his forehead and over his temples.

Mom followed Errol to the Pediatrics ICU, where I would lie heavily sedated for days. I had my own room, and Mom made herself comfortable on a reclining chair. Her fingers gripped my limp hand. There were no stuffed animals lining my bed or under my arm this time. The operation was over, but the process had only just begun.

I didn't wake up from surgery until four days after the doctors completed their work. I couldn't figure out if it was day or night—it felt like time had stopped. Instead of a clock ticking, I heard monitors all around me, beeping and chirping, keeping time with their own strangely melodic tune. Other machines around my bed made a steady humming noise, and I could almost feel that humming traveling through the wires attached to my skin and into my body. I hummed with pain.

The air was still and I could hear muffled echoes at a distance. Then I heard them move toward me, closer and closer, until they were hovering over my body. I was too scared to open my eyes. I didn't need to see in order to understand what was going on around me. I could feel the nurses' presence. My mind felt clouded, but my senses worked on overdrive, trying to regain their bearings while my brain sluggishly tried to catch up. I felt, smelled, heard, and tasted everything, all at once. And all of it was amplified.

A nurse rustled around in his pocket and tore open a package. A syringe, I was pretty sure, then an alcohol swab. The powerful odor stung my sinuses. Then I felt him guide the syringe into my IV and I knew it was full of more methadone. The drug bit at my veins as it flowed under my skin. Certain medications produce physical sensations. Some are cold and others are hot. Some tingle while others jolt.

Sometimes I feel like I could write the manual.

I heard him shuffle around in his pocket again, this time for the medical tape and scissors. Gently he secured the IV wires to my hand with an extra layer of tape. I could feel him looking at me, wondering why a teenage girl would *voluntarily* put herself through all of this.

I didn't feel like a teenage girl. I felt like a fifteen-year-old warrior. There was nothing innocent about my pain.

Once again, I could feel the kind nurse's eyes take in my motionless body.

He probably felt bad for me.

Maybe he knew me. Was this nurse one of my mom's hospital friends? Maybe I'd met him before. I wondered if he knew how much I wanted this.

The pain in my legs felt twisted and cruel. The sensations contradicted themselves—hot, then cold, sharp pains followed by a dull, achy numbness. The chilly hospital room felt like it had become even colder in the minutes (or had it been hours?) since I first woke up. I swore I could feel my drilled and severed bones shiver and my muscles clamp around them. It was a shocking, terrifying sensation, but I couldn't scream. The force of the sound exiting my mouth would be too painful to bear. All I could do was remain still, keep my eyes shut, and allow the tears to fall down my cheeks. The nurse, still beside my bed, gently lifted them away with his fingertips. His hands felt smooth and young. I silently wished that he'd stay.

As I listened to him sift through a drawer, I noticed that my throat was so swollen from the long intubation that I could barely swallow. And a peculiar, thick smell was everywhere. It was inside my mouth, coating my tongue, and filling my head. The scents of bleach and laundry detergent that lingered on my blankets mixed with the smells of plastic and rubbing alcohol—a sickening perfume of my surgery. Once I noticed it, I couldn't stop smelling it.

I felt the nurse leave. Finally, I lifted my heavy eyelids just a bit. Through the open sliver, I noticed the light in the hallway illuminating another profile. The rest of the room remained dark. Sitting at the end of my hospital bed with his head in his hands was my dad. His outline glowed in the dim hallway light. When I opened my eyes just a millimeter wider, I saw that he was crying.

Dad looked crumpled, defeated. He never talked about blaming himself for giving me half of the diastrophic dysplasia gene that caused my dwarfism. I could only imagine that was what he was feeling now. Despite being able to fix damn near anything placed in front of him, he could never fix me.

My father felt a different kind of pain than I did in the ICU. He hated himself for not having enough strength to stand up and voice his discontent about my decision to have surgery. He damned my mother for not only also supporting my choice, but also encouraging me to go after my independence at any cost. Mom understood what I yearned for, but Dad never saw a need for it. In his mind, no matter how old I got, he would simply take care of his little girl for as long as she needed. I think his pain, ultimately, was worse than my own.

I felt my eyelids get heavy again and slowly close, almost without my consent. Then, like magic, all the sensations that had been whirling around in my body gently floated away. My pain lifted and I sank deeper into the mattress below. It was as if I was drowning under heavy, crashing waves, but I finally had relief from the stifling pain, and that was all that mattered. Everything went weightless, including my mind.

The methadone had finally started to work.

A few hazy, foggy days later, a physical therapist arrived at my hospital bed. Dr. Mortimer had sent her. I was told I had to stand for the first time since my bones had been surgically broken. She insisted I move my legs to prevent blood clots and to get the circulation flowing again after remaining immobile for so long.

I begged for more time but was quickly denied.

Gently but purposefully, the therapist swung my metal-clad legs around to the side of my bed and hoisted me to my feet. My body insisted that everyone hear how badly it hurt.

More rabid animal than teenage girl, I screamed, jerked, shook, and cried. The sounds caused my mom to well up with tears and the assistant nurse gripped my mom's hand tightly, if not to support my mother so much as herself. My cries flooded the room and reached out into the hallway.

I felt like an anchor being thrown off a ship: heavy, paralyzed by my own weight, and unable to change a damn thing about it. The sweat developing on my feet did nothing to create stability for my body on the cold floor. It felt much harder under my feet than I ever remembered it feeling before.

Someone thrust a walker in front of me and the assistant nurse struggled to fit my legs with their pins between its metal bars. The walker clicked and clanged against the black half-moons fastened around my shins. I felt every vibration. I was unable to stand without literally hanging on to the therapist, and I couldn't adjust my posture from an involuntary slump. Just standing upright was more difficult and more painful than I ever could have imagined.

The skin around the wires in my feet ripped. It made my spine flex, my pupils dilate. Even the distinct, sharp feeling of adrenaline pulsing through my body didn't seem to help me. All I could do was stand and endure it.

"Okay, okay! I did it! Let me back on the bed! Get me back on the bed!" I screamed.

"One more minute. Try to breathe for one minute, Tiffanie. You can *do* this!" the therapist said.

It seemed far too easy for her to say as she held tightly on to me so I wouldn't fall forward. She was trained to be loud and demanding in times like these—so expertly unmoved by agony.

"I did it already! God, please! I did it already!" After days of adjusting to the pain of staying still, I had to bear the far more excruciating pain of movement and learning how to function all over again.

"Breathe, Tiff! Breathe! You have to breathe before we can lift you back on the bed . . ."

"Please! Please! *Please!*" I screamed over and over.

"Breathe!"

"C'mon, Tiff, you can do this!" my mom chimed in.

"If you can scream, you can breathe!" the therapist shouted over me.

"I'm breathing, damn it!" I cried. Sounds exited my mouth that I never knew I could make. My chest heaved violently up and down, unable to keep up with the emotions inside me. The pain was excruciating but all I could think about was completing the task so that the torture would stop. Quitting wasn't an option.

My eyes darted at everyone in the room. No one moved. They waited, gripping one another for support. They braced themselves for the possibility that I was going to crack and maybe even admit that I had made a horrible mistake having this surgery.

This was my first battle, not only to prove that I made the right decision to undergo bone-lengthening again, but to also prove I could take responsibility for my actions.

I decided to fight.

I took a deep breath and pictured an imaginary figure standing before me. I stared at that little girl, barely four feet tall, sitting on an egg crate in front of a room full of students, being forced to hear all the things that made her different.

I didn't blink. I stopped screaming. I just kept staring at that little girl I conjured in front of me. She was everything I hated. She was my enemy. Despite the pain thrashing inside my body, I released the hardest breath of my life.

A second later, the nursing assistant and the therapist lifted me quickly back on the hospital bed. They smiled with relief and covered me with a blanket. I had won.

I sat trembling, trying to catch my breath, staring at my legs. I needed a moment by myself. Mom followed everyone out of the room and stopped in the hallway. She thought she was out of earshot, but I could hear her sobbing and speaking quietly with one of the nurses. She didn't want me to see her, my pillar of strength, collapse.

Slowly, I pulled the blanket aside and gawked at the pins sticking out of my skin. I envisioned how they must look fastened down into my bones. Underneath all the muscles and nerves, I imagined them looking very raw.

What would everything look like when all the pins, nails, and wires were removed? What scars would they leave? How would those marks be different from those that all my other surgeries left behind?

Some of the scars would overlap, I thought to myself. Some would be deep and rooted, while others would just be pink knots

on the surface. They would be engraved, crescent-shaped reminders telling a tale of pain, determination, and happiness. My battle
wounds—complex markings more original and intricate than
any tattoo. Then, clearing her throat, Mom made her way back
into the room. She approached the bed and took my hand in
hers.

"You did good, Tiffie. You did so good."

I felt I had done nothing special. I did what I was told to do.

"It took you a bit, but you got control. That's what you have
to do from now on, gain control."

"I didn't think I would have to feel anything like that in my
life," I told her.

"You have a new life now. This is what you have to feel in
your new life."

I said nothing, just relieved that the pain was over, for now.

"You did good," she repeated. "I knew you could do it. I'm
proud of you."

"Why?" I said softly, in between shaky breaths.

"Because nowhere during that godawful experience did you
once say, 'I can't do this anymore.'"

Several days later, I came home from the hospital. The sweet,
familiar smell of cinnamon buns filled the house. I spent the
night on our hideously upholstered sectional pullout couch. It
was convenient, low to the ground, and I could watch TV with
my family (or even all night if I wanted to). Mom stacked mountains of pillows under my legs to ease the pain.

Just like when I had pins in as a kid, Mom sat beside me with
two plates in her hand. I picked at my food while she made quick
work of hers. I'd left my taste buds somewhere in the hospital, sedated and unresponsive. With my mom by my side, I filled my days
attempting then perfecting bed transfers, moving from the couch

to a reclining blue chair. I watched National Geographic tornado specials on VHS, but the drugs never let me get through them in their entirety. I was constantly in limbo between sleep and reality. I worked on developing an appetite after all those days in the hospital and took in my surroundings at home as best I could. Despite the sweet smell of cinnamon sugar hanging in the air, my home felt strangely foreign, as if I had been gone for years.

My couch setup worked for a day or two, but eventually, my moderate level of comfort deteriorated.

As I tried to drift off to sleep one of my first few nights back home, the autumn air blew in through our living room window and kept my forehead and face cool. The rest of my body felt like it was burning up. I tried so hard to sleep, but to no avail. Each time I moved, even the tiniest bit, my body worked up so much heat that the sheets stuck to my skin. My shoulders ached from the pressure of being pinned to the couch—now my bed—for hours on end.

It's amazing how many noises you can hear at night when you're struggling to sleep. Frogs and insects that never seem to make a peep in the daytime suddenly can't shut up. To me the crickets were the worst. They seemed to grow louder and louder with each passing minute. What could they possibly have to drone on about all night? I felt like the Grinch: I was restless and angry from all the noise, noise, *noise!*

There was just as much of a racket inside my house as there was outside, anyway. The refrigerator rattled and then began to hum every six minutes. I timed it. And then there was this random scratching inside the walls, like something was trying to get in. Does *anything* ever sleep? I wondered. By eleven p.m., I was ready to drift off. But amid the cricket-refrigerator-house-settling chorus, one a.m. appeared on my clock before I knew it.

Then two a.m. came and went.

Three a.m. rolled by.

By five a.m., the crickets had finally started to grow quiet, but the sun was rising over the nearly bare trees. The light was somehow louder than all the noises combined. It wasn't until six a.m. that I finally figured out why it was so incredibly difficult for me to fall asleep.

I couldn't roll over.

I wanted desperately to turn on my side and pull my legs up under me as I'd done so casually over the past fifteen years. But thanks to the metal halos around my legs, I couldn't comfortably snuggle under my sheets. I couldn't throw one leg up over a pillow or turn and plop on my stomach with a foot dangling off the bed. Just finding a comfortable sleeping position was a luxury I had taken for granted.

I had no choice but to sleep on my back. Worse yet, I had to sleep like that every night for at least a year until my entire procedure was over. This was just another surprise included with the package of the surgery.

Welcome home, Tiff.

By seven a.m., I was desperate. My father's alarm clock had just gone off and echoed throughout the entire house. He was beginning his day when I never had the opportunity to end mine. As he came down the stairs and into the living room, I noticed he was frowning. His eyes looked sad at the sight of what was before him.

Me.

"You're still up?" he asked.

"No, no, I'm fine. I just heard the alarm clock."

He saw right through me.

"Can I get you anything? Can I fix anything?"

"My waist is a little hot, but my feet are really cold," I told him. They were always cold. It was a numb cold. And they were so swollen.

He walked toward me slowly. Then he folded the covers away from my upper body and grabbed a blanket that was tossed over the blue chair and placed it softly across my feet and legs.

"There. How's that?"

I smiled at him in response.

Later that morning from somewhere upstairs, I heard my dad ask my mom, "What if . . . ?" again and again. No longer did he ask how things were. He became more concerned with how things were going to be.

"What if she came home too soon?" I heard him ask. They must have thought I was asleep and they gradually lost track of their volume, speaking louder and louder.

"She's fine. Dr. Mortimer wouldn't allow that," Mom assured him.

"What if she wants a snack later on and we're not home?"

"We'll put some snacks on her table by her chair," she said. "I already have that covered."

"What if she needs to use the bathroom? Is she going to use the bedpan during the whole recovery process?"

Mom paused. She couldn't answer that as simply and optimistically as she answered the others.

Dad repeated: "What if she has to use the bathroom, Robin?"

"She'll walk." Mom tried to hide her uncertainty.

"Walk?"

"She's going to have to."

"How the hell is she going to walk, Robin?"

"She'll do it. People do it all the time."

"Other people didn't have her surgery."

"She's not the only one to have this operation, Gerry," Mom said with a sigh. "Dr. Mortimer wants her to walk. It helps the lengthening process."

"I didn't hear him say that."

"You didn't hear him say that because you were too busy avoiding the idea. Now you hear me saying it. People break their legs, get pins and external fixators in, and they learn to function. They have to walk. She has to walk."

My dad raised his voice. "Other people break *a* leg! She has both legs wrapped up in those *things*!"

"So?"

"*So?*"

I could tell my dad was stunned at the way Mom dismissed his worries. "So don't you think you should have thought about all this before you jumped in the Jeep and went to the hospital?" he shouted.

"She *did* think about it."

"Not enough!"

"Believe me, she thought about it plenty!"

"How is she going to function with them?" Dad snapped.

"How is she going to function *without* them?"

Their argument was like a tennis match, with each of my parents trying to score a point on the other. It sounded a lot like the ones I remembered from my childhood.

"The same way other people with disabilities go through life," Dad yelled. "They have help! They have help without surgery."

"Maybe she doesn't want help!"

"She'll take my help. She doesn't need to reach pedals in a car. I'll take her where she wants to go."

My mom sighed and the conversation stopped momentarily. I craned my neck to hear them.

"It's not just about a car," Mom continued more softly. "It's about independence."

"*I'll* help her."

"And when you're dead and gone? And when I'm dead and gone? What then, Gerry?"

My dad said nothing. There was more silence. Then I heard him stomp across the hardwood floor in the master bedroom.

"You're not going to live forever, Gerry!" Mom called out after him.

"Yes, I am!" he shouted back. It was an absurd retort, but his frustration had gotten the best of him.

Dad rushed down the stairs and flung the front door wide open, and seconds later the sound of it slamming shut echoed throughout the house.

I watched out the front window as Dad picked up the leaf blower. Our lawn wasn't cluttered with leaves. It wasn't speckled with any remains of the season, in fact, because he had cleaned it all up the day before. Yet he still turned on the obnoxiously loud machine.

Dad moved it quickly side to side, aiming at anything in sight—pebbles, grass clippings, freshly dropped acorn tops. His frustration and anger blew everything in the yard away. But he couldn't do anything about the pain. He gripped the leaf blower as if he were strangling the very life out of it, and I studied his face. He was beet red, with his bottom lip tucked under his upper lip.

I was no longer the only one in my family going through this surgery. I wasn't the only one fighting.

I heard my mom coming down the stairs and I turned away from the window and faced her when she came into view. She didn't have to say anything. I knew what needed to be done.

There would no longer be the comfort of a bedpan or the security of having Mom to help me make it to the toilet in time. There would no longer be yelling for help or waiting until the last minute to go. From that point on, there was just me, and the distance I had to travel to the bathroom.

Taking it easy was officially over.

"You should try now," she said as if reading my mind—or assuming I'd heard her fighting with my dad.

I glanced at my juice cup. There was just enough left to swallow a Percocet. The pain would be impossible to ignore. I hated taking pills, but they would be my modest level of protection against the wires barbed through my feet.

I didn't know how long it was going to take me to reach the bathroom or what it would feel like to walk. I had taken just a few little steps from the bed to the recliner and that had been pure hell.

It's hard to explain the difficulty of forcing yourself to do something that you know will cause you pain. Somehow I allowed myself to let Mom grab the metal rungs around my legs, lift them, and then place them over the side of the bed. She did it very slowly. Then she stepped away and waited. I struggled to balance just sitting on the edge of my bed. My back muscles were so weak from constantly lying down.

When I lowered myself to the floor, the pain in my legs was immediate. It was sharp, like a million jagged pieces of glass slicing through my muscles. I felt the blood rush down to my legs and swirl inside my feet. I felt like they were going to explode from the inside out. Part of me wanted them to explode so they wouldn't be there anymore.

I closed my eyes and accepted the pain. I swallowed hard and took one quick glance at the distance to the hallway. It seemed like a mile away. Every bit of it was going to hurt.

I gripped the walker my mom handed me so tightly that my knuckles turned white. With one quick pull, I yanked myself up onto my feet. What I felt next made me wish for something I never expected.

I wanted to die.

I wanted the out-of-body experience people talk about on TV, the floating sensation. I wanted the weightlessness, because everything was too heavy to bear. I wanted out of my body. But I was stuck, yet again, inside of it. I had no choice but to force myself to accept that, too.

"Use your arms as much as you can," Mom said.

She sounded awfully far away for being right at my side.

"Breathe, honey."

I felt like the wind had been knocked out of me.

My first steps were hardly steps at all. They were more like swings. I saw my mom tense up as I took my first one. She relaxed a little when she saw me do it successfully.

I released the air I was holding in. It came out like I had a hundred flaming birthday candles in front of me. Then I pushed the walker forward a bit. I lifted myself again and swung my legs forward.

I didn't want to cry out in pain for my dad to hear.

My mom had calculated that the bathroom was about fourteen steps away. The toilet, my goal, was twenty steps away. I had only done two steps, and already the sweat was gathering all over my body. I wanted to quit.

I had eighteen more steps to go and eighteen more reasons to hate my life and regret my choice to have surgery.

But I lifted and swung again.

Again.

And again.

Then I had to sit.

Mom hurried over with the small black desk chair where I used to do my homework. When I sat, I looked back at the couch and at the distance I had just created. Through the hot tears burning my eyes, I saw that my undertaking was nothing more than baby steps. But I also felt like I'd taken a massive leap away from weakness, and that made me smile. Suddenly, those horrible remaining fourteen steps became fourteen reasons why I needed to keep going.

"I'm going to the toilet," I said without hesitation.

"All right," my mom responded. "We're going to the toilet."

I grabbed the walker once more, pulled myself up, and stood. The shock of pain returned.

New things began to hurt. My back muscles seared. My shoulders pinched, and the palms of my hands felt raw from holding the walker so tightly. More frustrating than all the pain, though, was the tingling in my bladder.

More tears gathered in my eyes and fell down my face. They blended with the beads of sweat sliding down my cheeks. But I never cried out loud. I pushed the walker forward. Then swung through. Over and over I did this, creating a rhythm.

I inhaled, leaned on my hands, lifted my body, and swung forward. Then I lowered myself down onto the ground, exhaled, and pushed the walker.

I inhaled and started all over again. All the while, my mom remained silent. There was only the sound of my struggle. Each time I placed a foot on the floor, the wires pulled at my flesh. I glanced down and saw the skin rise up the wires when I put weight on my feet, then slide back down as I lifted. It stung and burned with every inch.

I swung, lowered myself back to the floor, and exhaled.

My skin tore and rose in little shreds back up the wires and my bladder felt like it was filling up with rocks as my gut extended outward.

"I *really* have to go!"

"Squeeze!" Mom replied.

I couldn't squeeze my legs together with the metal halos in the way, so I sucked in my belly and pressed on. Somewhere between the pain and the hatred for my body, I had entered the hallway and stood in the bathroom doorway. I was almost there.

I picked up the pace as best I could. I could feel my heart racing with anticipation and hope. Happiness, too: I could finally see the toilet! There it was, ready for me: sweet relief, a goal, and a huge accomplishment. That toilet was my proof that I could win any personal battle.

I somehow managed to move even faster. My adrenaline kicked in as drainage leaked out of the wounds around the pins. I could feel it seeping out and spiraling down the backs of my legs. I didn't care. I didn't want to acknowledge anything—not even the tiny bloody footprints I was making on the tile.

"Am I supposed to leak this much?" I asked my mom while looking straight ahead. I felt more warm fluid come down my inner thighs. A lot more.

She didn't respond. She just placed a hand on my shoulder, as if telling me to stop.

Puzzled, I looked down.

I had peed all over myself.

My mind kept telling me I could hold it a few minutes longer, but my bladder had given up. My shins were too numb to feel it, but my heart certainly did when I looked down to see my light pink boxer shorts turning a deep shade of purple. I was so close. I could lean forward and touch the rim of the toilet seat. I could kick it if I had the strength to raise my leg. I was that damn close.

The feeling of stones in my gut dissolved as I stood in my own urine. The puddle collected around my bare feet and in between each toe. I was almost sixteen years old and I had just gone to the bathroom all over the floor.

"It's sterile," my mom said reassuringly as she rushed to grab some towels. "What goes in must come out, honey!"

I didn't care. I was mortified, and so angry with myself. How the hell was I unable to make it to the toilet on time? I was almost sixteen! A sixteen-year-old who *wet her pants*. What was wrong with me? The surgery, the pain, the pins—there was no justification for what went down. I simply should have made it.

That was when I let myself cry. My tears fell to the floor and my grip on the walker loosened. My feet began to slide out from under me and my courage and will felt like they were slipping away, too.

I screamed as I started to fall. The tile was so slippery and I barely had the ability to put weight on my feet to begin with. I struggled to pull my legs back under my body. My feet dragged against the tile floor, pulling my skin even farther from the wires. I looked down to see blood leaking into the mix. Little girls are supposed to be made of sugar, spice, and everything nice. That day I saw what I was made of: sweat, blood, tears, and urine. My days of innocently playing with my Barbie in her frilly white wedding gown were over. It was nothing but piss and vinegar for me now, and stained purple shorts.

"Lift up," Mom said. She was so calm. She helped lift me as much as she could.

"Use your arms and lift up your body so I can get the towel under you. Just stand on it, honey; you won't slip."

I closed my eyes as she used another towel to dry my legs, gently patting in between the wires. She pulled down my soaked shorts and I lifted myself up again, barely, as she slid another towel under my feet. I kept crying and tried to turn back around and head toward my bed.

"Where are you going?" Mom asked.

"I . . . already . . . went," I gasped, crying harder now.

"No. You said you were going to go to the bathroom, and you're going to do it."

"I want to go lie down."

"Are you crying?" my mom asked me. She was on her knees wiping up the mess, but she lifted her shoulders to face me. "Are those tears?"

"I already went!" I shouted, hysterical and uncooperative.

"You do *not* cry!" Her voice deepened like those of the drill instructors we'd admired on base years before. "Get angry!"

"What? Stop screaming at me," I whimpered.

"Stop your crying! You said you were going to walk to that toilet and you're going to walk to that toilet. You have two steps left!"

"It's all over the floor!"

"You have two steps left, God damn it! Take them!" She screamed louder than I did. "Take them! I know my daughter. I know you can do it!"

I didn't know what to say.

"It's only urine," she shouted. "Do you hear me? Get angry and take those steps!"

You can take the officer out of the military, but you can't take the military out of my mom.

Just then, I heard the front door close and my father walking back into the house. He'd obviously heard all the yelling.

"What's going on?" he shouted, and I heard him walking toward the bathroom.

My mother reacted without missing a beat.

"Nothing! Mind your own business!" she shouted, and she slammed the bathroom door shut. I may have been in a seriously embarrassing predicament, but I still deserved to keep my dignity, and my mother saw to it that I kept it.

She was trying to distract me from the scene. She was trying to make me tough, to thicken my skin. She was building me up from the pit into which I wanted to fall. It worked. I cannot thank her enough for that.

So I stopped crying. I gripped my walker again, and with every ounce of strength I had left, I took the remaining two steps to the toilet. Then I sat down on it. I'd finally made it—more or less.

When my mom finished cleaning up my legs and feet, I reached back my hand and flushed the toilet anyway. It was my victory siren. I flushed away the entire ordeal. I actually smiled as I let the whole experience swirl away down into the sewer. Somehow, it sucked away all the embarrassment and left me with a sense of accomplishment, pride, and total relief that it was all over with, and I could go back to my bed on the couch and relax. Until the next time I had to use the bathroom.

"Gerry!" my mom called. "Come help her, please!" She opened the door and stuck her head out to make sure my dad was on his way.

He'd never left the other side of the door.

"You did enough for now, Tiffie," Mom said.

I happily let my father reach under my arms with one of his, tuck the other underneath my thighs, and carry me back to the couch. It never felt better.

Everything finally became weightless.

I napped until two thirty that afternoon and woke up to the phone ringing. It was Mike, and he could tell right away that I had been through an ordeal.

"What's up?" he asked in that caring, wonderful voice.

I told him. I told him *everything*.

"But you did it, right?" he asked.

"Um, no. I went on the floor," I replied simply.

"Don't care about that. You did it, right? You made it?"

"Well, yeah, but—"

Mike interrupted me. "So what's the problem?"

"I don't think you heard me. I said I peed all over myself. I peed on the *floor*, Michael." I didn't expect him to dismiss it all so easily. But Mike just didn't care. Part of me wanted his sympathy.

But Mike wouldn't be the one to give that to me. By not showering me with sympathy, he was refusing to acknowledge what made us different.

He was just my best friend, calling to hear about my accomplishment of the day.

# CHAPTER 9

# You're Gonna Be the One
# That Saves Me

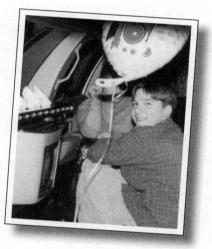

Mike in the limo at my sweet sixteen
birthday celebration.

THE DAILY ROUTINE I dreaded most during the bone-lengthening
process was pin care. Not even the constant physical therapy was
worse, because once I was pumped up to stretch or do range-of-
motion routines, my blood scorched through my veins and em-
powered me to work.

Nothing pumped me up for pin care. With more than a dozen
pins protruding from my legs, I had to clean them—every single
one of them—twice a day.

It not only hurt, it was messy and irritating and tediously re-
petitive. The process took about forty-five minutes each time.

First there was the task of gathering supplies from the linen closet: a blue absorbent pad, sterile saline, a plastic presealed cup, quarter-sized octagon-shaped sponges, sterile cotton swabs that looked like giant Q-tips, and hydrogen peroxide. Then there was the prep work.

First I filled a cup with saline. Next my mom lifted my legs and placed the pad underneath them to catch the liquid that would inevitably roll off, and the big Q-tips went into the cup. Then we had to remove all of the little octagon-shaped sponges that were anchored around each pin from the night before. It was painstaking. Worse yet, some of the sponges dried to the pin sites, like clingy stubborn little squeegees, wrapped around the pins. There was no choice but to rip them away. Pin care was a necessary evil. There was just no way around it. Eventually, I found a way around some of the sticky scenarios. Ever a control freak and insistent on doing things myself, I poured hydrogen peroxide over each pin and let the mini sponges absorb it until they were too soaked to stick. The cold peroxide made my thigh muscles rise up and flex around the pins—which was almost as painful as a muscle spasm. This was only the beginning. Each pin took four Q-tips. I dipped each swab into the saline and wiped away any scabs, making sure also to push my skin gently down and away from the pin. Twice a day I was a living, breathing, barely walking maintenance machine. And I bitched and moaned, winced and clenched my teeth the whole time.

Coping with pain in my house meant one of two things. If you could fix it, you did so and moved on. If you refused to fix it, you were on your own. "Suffer, then!" Mom would say—the choices were to suffer or fix it. Given those two options, I did my best to "get a straw," as Mom was so fond of saying, and suck it up.

While going through the tedious motions one day, a TV ad

for a car—a BMW Z3—caught my gaze and wouldn't let go. The car was beautiful, sexy, and intriguing. The driver looked carefree and limitless. It was the greatest thing I'd ever seen on television. Everything about that vehicle exemplified independence and I desperately wanted it.

"DiDonato. Tiffanie DiDonato," Dad teased in his best James Bond impression. "The ultimate driving machine," he said, smiling. A car fanatic with a '66 GTO and a Corvette of his own, Dad found it particularly amusing that his daughter, who never expressed an interest in automobiles, had somehow managed to eye one of the most expensive ones out there. I think it made him proud.

What's more, that little roadster opened a whole new realm of motivation for me. It blew me away. As I turned my pins, I visualized myself driving it. Day after day, I became one millimeter closer to reaching its pedals. I wanted more motivation to keep pushing through my rehabilitation. I requested free catalogs from clothing retailers like Girlfriends and dELiA*s. My parents even allowed me to order a few outfits. I hung them on the bathroom door or in our dining room entranceway. While I continued to struggle with walking to the bathroom and the sensation of my skin rolling up and down the wires, I pushed the feeling away by imagining what the material would feel like on legs longer than the ones I currently had. That November, I was approaching my first full one-inch mark—and my sixteenth birthday. Suddenly, the same clothes that compelled me to work hard became visual reminders of what I couldn't wear.

My body wasn't capable of celebrating much of anything yet. But Mike disagreed. Over the course of several phone calls he began his campaign to sell me on a sweet sixteen celebration.

At first, Mike was subtle and cute in his efforts.

He would call me and play Oasis's "Wonderwall" on his guitar. I always closed my eyes during the line, "'Cause maybe . . . you're gonna be the one that saves me," thinking about how much comfort Mike brought me by just being there. Then the birthday badgering began. "What do you have planned next week?" he'd asked casually.

"Nothing."

"I think it's someone's birthday next week, too, but I forget who . . ."

"Oh? Sounds like a problem you have there." I played right into his little game, just as I always did.

"If it was your birthday next week, what would you want to do for it?"

"If it was *my* birthday, *I* would do nothing."

"Nothing?" I could tell he was gearing up to jump down my throat. "Tiff, you can't *not* celebrate your sixteenth birthday!"

"I thought you forgot whose birthday it was," I said with the slightest giggle, holding the phone close to me.

"And I thought you'd want to do something cool."

I glanced at the Girlfriends catalog on my hospital table and felt a pang of envy over the teenage model looking so carefree and happy in her brand-new outfit. She was ready to party. I was not.

"Well, my ball gown is still at the cleaner's. So naturally that puts a damper on my exciting plans," I joked.

"Do you always have to be a wiseass?"

"It's better than being a dumb-ass."

"Tiff, seriously."

"Mike"—I matched his serious tone—"I *am* serious. Last week I pissed my pants, my appetite isn't fully back yet, and I'm stuck in plus-size men's boxers instead of pants."

"Excuses, excuses," he scolded. "You can't just sit in that chair for your birthday."

As the week passed, Mike started to get more aggressive with his approach over the phone.

"Decide what you want to do for your birthday?" he asked.

"I want to relax," I insisted.

"Why?"

"How am I going to do anything else?"

"Who cares how you do it, just do something that doesn't involve the recliner."

"I don't want to. I'll be happy staying home."

"Your mom wants to go to dinner, I bet."

"I'm sure she does."

He paused before speaking again, this time as if he'd uncovered a hidden secret.

"Oh, I get it. You're afraid to leave the house."

*"What?"*

"I don't believe it. Tiffanie DiDonato is a chicken shit."

"I am not!"

"And you're selfish. Your parents probably want to take you out, and you're saying no."

"Shut up. You're being mean."

"Nope. I'm being honest. And I'm right. *I'm right!*" He was practically screaming.

"No, you really aren't."

"You won't leave the house because you're afraid! You don't want people to see you! You think you're hideous!"

"Mike, stop!"

"Stop being a scared little bitch!" Subtlety, with Mike, often found itself leaping out the nearest window.

"Stop yelling at me!"

"Accept yourself!"

Then there was silence.

"You're going to let the fear of other people prevent you from doing shit. This is what started the whole surgery idea in the first place," Mike began again.

"You have it backwards."

"I thought this procedure was supposed to help you."

"It is!"

"It's keeping you in the house."

"I have metal pins and nails in me, Michael!" I was angry now, raising my voice in a way I never had with him before. "I can't even lift up my legs!"

"So?"

"Mike, what the hell do you want me to do?" My eyes watered with frustration.

"Prove this surgery is working."

"It's not complete yet! How am I supposed to do that?"

"Prove you're happy with your decision."

"I *am* happy! Can't you tell in my voice? *I'm fucking happy!*" I attempted to muster a pleasant tone. But Mike knew just what buttons to push to get me fired up.

"Then go out to dinner," he said calmly.

"How will that prove anything?"

"Go out to dinner," he insisted.

"Mike, listen to me," I argued.

"Go out to dinner." He wouldn't budge. Anything I tried to say was met with the same line: "Go out to dinner."

"Fine!"

"Great. Love you!" he said as sweet as could be, as if no argument had happened at all. He said it sweetly because he won.

"Love you, too, damn it." Part of me wanted him to win.

The next few times Mike called, he asked to speak directly to my mom. It wasn't too suspicious, because he often liked to make small talk with my parents. Unconcerned, I passed the phone to my mom, but I did squeeze in one question.

"Are you coming to dinner with us?"

"No. Celebrate with your mom and dad. I'll come over after."

"Fine. Be that way."

And that was that. Despite our yelling and name-calling, Mike knew me pretty well. Underneath my tough exterior, I really was afraid of people seeing my pins. Yes, I had made the choice to undergo the procedure to help change not only the way people saw me, but also the way I saw myself. But what if I scared children? What if I went out to celebrate my birthday, and I permanently damaged a child's innocence with the sight of these things? They were pretty disgusting, after all. Even I had a hard time looking at them. If I was a child and I saw pins drilled through someone's legs, I'd go running to my mom crying!

I didn't want to flaunt my choice. Not until it was all over with, anyway. I didn't want to worry about draping a blanket over my entire lower half the whole night. And the dress I had always wanted to wear for a very special occasion—a velvet, emerald green one with sheer long sleeves I had bought with Dad at Filene's—was meant to go to the knee. *Not* the ankle. How could I ever wear something beautiful like that with legs like mine?

All I could do was trust in my mom that she would create something to match it, as she'd promised, so I could dine comfortably. For hours, she sat upstairs in her room, the motor of her sewing machine spinning away. Just before she revealed her big project, Mom brought down some of her makeup and a mirror and placed them on my hospital table.

"Here," she said with a smile. "I think the amethyst shadow would bring out the brown in your eyes the most." She slid the shadow across my table with a thimble-covered finger and went back upstairs.

Fooling around with the makeup, I was reminded of all the times I'd stood atop my makeshift ladder in Mom's room, playing with her jewelry. This time was very different. Now I could reach my earlobes, my bangs, and even the top of my head. As I swept the deep purple powder across my eyelids, I smiled to myself.

From upstairs, Mom called out to me.

"Here it comes!"

She was so proud of herself. I knew by the expression on her face that even if what she'd made turned out to be a mess, I would have to at least fake a smile. Hurting my mom's feelings would sting far more than being seen in a monstrosity.

When she revealed what she had made to cover my pins, all my worries about people staring at me faded away. The dress was beautiful. Mom had somehow found the exact same fabric— emerald green velvet—and attached it to the hem of my original dress.

It had pouf, but it wasn't too puffy. It was narrow at the waist and flowed to elegantly cover my legs. There was even a little zipper on the side so that I could wrap my legs up tighter in case they got cold. I had a ball gown after all.

"I love it!" I squealed. "Thank you! Thank you, thank you!"

"See? I'm good for something," Mom said with a wink as she brought it over to me.

Little did she know that I thought she was good at everything.

The gown slid on and over the pins with ease. It gave my legs warmth against the crisp November air without making me too hot. With my matching green satin hair tie in place, I was officially ready to celebrate my birthday over a nice dinner. Maybe agreeing to go out wouldn't be such a bad thing after all.

"Ready, pumpkin?" my dad asked.

"Ready." I smiled at him and lifted my arms for him to pick me up.

"Let's go pig out," he said with a wink. He scooped me up into his arms and carried me out the front door. That night, Dad had an extra bounce in his step. To me it was amazing, considering how much more I must have weighed with all that metal attached to me. I think he was just happy to finally see me out of the house.

As we made our way down the front porch stairs, I was shocked to notice what was waiting in the driveway.

"A stretch limo!" I shrieked. "I thought we were going in your Jeep, Mom!"

"Wait, wait, let me get in front of you!" she told my dad. "I want to see her face!" Mom hurried out in front of him, her high heels clattering on the pavement.

"Ready?" she asked me.

I nodded.

"We're ready!" Mom announced, tapping on the roof of the limo with the palm of her hand.

The limo door opened, and there, with a sweet sixteen balloon and a big smile on his face, was Mike.

"Happy birthday, babes," he said, beaming.

From behind him, Megan, Jen, and another friend of mine from English class, named Erin, chimed in. "Happy birthday!" they all screamed, throwing their hands in the air.

"Oh my God!" I shouted. Mom clapped her hands and cheered. I'd never seen her happier.

Mike had helped plan the whole thing.

As Dad eased me into the limo, I had tears in my eyes.

"Don't ruin your eye makeup," Jen said, adding another thick coat of gloss over her lips.

"We'll see you all there," Mom called to me.

"You're not coming in, too?" I asked, shouting out the door.

"No, no. This is for you. We'll follow in the car." Before I could argue that there was more than enough room, Mom shut the door. Mike seated himself next to me. "Are they under there?" Mike asked, gesturing at my legs as the limo began to pull down the driveway.

"My legs? No, I left them in the house. I'll have the doctor put them back on when the night's over," I joked.

Mike playfully nudged me, and his leg slightly brushed up against mine, tapping one of the pins.

"Oh, shit, did that hurt? I'm sorry!"

"I didn't feel anything," I said. "You're way more freaked out about these suckers than you were about the pins I had in my arms," I said, brushing it off.

"There weren't as many . . . in your arms," he stammered. "And they weren't as big."

"Mike isn't as tough as he puts on," Jen said, rolling her eyes and winking at him. "So, how've you been?"

"Tired, to be honest. It's hard to sleep. I can't roll over and get comfortable. But I'm good."

"Good! It's your birthday!" Jen squealed. She couldn't relate. "We need to celebrate!" She quickly turned on some upbeat club music. Soon, everyone was singing along, even quiet Erin.

"I have something for you," Mike said to me, reaching into one of the limo cubbyholes and pulling out a plastic container. Inside was a perfect pink Tiffany rose corsage. Red roses never appealed to me. Girls always talked so much about red roses, but I wanted something different, something uniquely me. And Mike got it. He got everything.

"I have to pin it on you. If I stick you, don't get pissed."

I laughed. "As you can see"—I pointed to the velvet ball gown covering my legs—"I'm used to being stuck with pins."

Mike didn't crack a smile.

"It was a joke."

"You can do better than that," he said as he pinned it perfectly above my heart.

When the limo hit a bump, instead of sticking me with a sharp pin, Mike ended up bumping into my legs again.

"Shit!" he shouted. "I'm sorry."

"Mike, it's fine. It doesn't hurt."

"No, dude. I should sit over there." He nodded toward the opposite end of the limo.

"It didn't hurt, Mike."

"I keep knocking into them. We're gonna go over more bumps in the road."

"It's all right, seriously. I promise." I patted the pins myself to show him it didn't hurt. He was so scared he would hurt me that he moved as far from me as he could.

After a half hour of music, jokes, and talking about what my life at home had been like thus far, the limo finally rolled to a stop at the Castle, a medieval-style restaurant that served pretty much anything suburban diners could imagine.

My excitement melted away when my dad took out the wheelchair from the trunk of the Pontiac and rolled me inside the restaurant. I wasn't upset by the wheelchair itself—I knew that no one expected me to walk. But I *was* embarrassed when the hostess had to clear a path for me to be wheeled through. I wanted to just go in smoothly and easily. Instead, a big production ensued.

People rotated in their chairs to watch. Some women seemed concerned for their purses; worried, perhaps, that I'd roll over them. Others set down their dinner forks, hunks of bread, or soup spoons and slid their chairs and their bodies awkwardly underneath their table to make room for me. I felt totally helpless sitting there and relying on everyone else to get me to my meal. Inside, I was criticizing the glacial pace with which our hostess moved chairs, slid empty tables to the side, and flattened bumps in area rugs so my wheelchair wouldn't get caught. Could she go any slower? Why not just place a giant spotlight on me and hire an announcer?

*Everyone move aside! Here comes Tiffanie and her medical issues!*

My embarrassment must have been written all over my face, because Mike spoke up.

"Hey, Tiff?"

I looked at him. He nodded and waved a hand in my direction, encouraging me to just let it go.

"Is this okay?" the hostess asked after what seemed to be a lifetime of rearranging the damn place. Why was she looking at me for approval? As if I would say, "No, this table sucks. Can we possibly find another table so we can create another scene? Perhaps at the other end of the restaurant?"

I looked to Mike again. He winked at me.

"It's great," I said. "Thank you."

"Wonderful. Enjoy your meal." She smiled and walked off.

Dinner was great, and so was the conversation. We exchanged "what we'll do when we're twenty-one" stories and laughed about memories we all shared before I left high school. No one focused on my surgery. I could be myself and experience a slice of normalcy with my birthday cake. I wanted the night to last forever.

On the way home, Mike still sat across from me inside the limo. When we arrived at my house, everyone gave me a hug good night and wished me one final happy birthday. We'd been smiling so much all night that our cheeks hurt, and my dad was no exception. It was a gift in itself to see him smiling like that. As he picked me up out of the limo and carried me up to our front door, I waved good-bye over his shoulder. By the time he placed me on the blue recliner, my body had had it. I was suddenly really tired, and the pain in my legs gradually began to breach the line of defense my pain pills had provided. The night had ended at the perfect time.

"I'll tell Mom you need more pain medicine when I go out there to bring in your gifts," Dad said. "You made out like a bandit tonight, huh?" I'd received a pink Victorian collectible bear, a desk lamp with glass beading, and, my favorite gift, a warm afghan with Winnie the Pooh on it. I felt thoroughly spoiled.

"I sure did, Dad, thank you," I replied. The pain kept growing. My muscles started to twitch, and the skin around my pins began to burn with irritation from sitting upright for hours in the wheelchair.

Outside, Mike climbed out of the limo.

"Mrs. D., you need help with that?" He took the Pooh blanket and the bear from my mom and made his way inside.

With my dad outside tipping the limo driver, Mike came into the living room. I felt the twitching and burning sensations fade away as he smiled at me.

"Hey."

"Hi," I said, smiling.

"Do you want the TV on?"

"Aren't you supposed to be going home?"

He flicked on the TV then made his way toward me. "I just thought I'd help a little before I go."

"MTV? Good choice," I said.

"Music is always good for you," he said, inching a bit closer. "Did you have fun tonight?"

"I didn't think I would, but I really, really did."

"Good. I was right." I could tell he was still a bit nervous around the pins. "Do you hurt right now?"

I paused. "No. I don't." The truth was, even if there was pain pulsing through me, I barely noticed it when he was around. "I have to turn them soon. You want to watch?"

He laughed. "Most girls ask me if I like them, or if I want to hang out. Leave it to you to ask if I'll watch you stretch your bones."

"I guess I'm not like most girls."

"No shit, dude." He smiled even wider.

"Well?" I continued. "Do you want to see how all this works?"

"No," he replied quickly.

I was mildly disappointed. I wanted to show him, but he was clearly too scared to see what I'd really been going through.

Instead, he placed the blanket carefully over my legs, as if it would make all the pins go away. Then he sat beside me. "I don't think I have time anyway. The limo is leaving soon."

I had always envisioned my first real kiss to be like those passionate, soap opera embraces. Where the guy struggles to admit how much he loves the girl, and just before she rushes in the opposite direction, he grabs her, pulls her into his arms while gazing into her eyes, and plants one on her.

That night, there may not have been any soap opera dramatics. But there were fireworks inside my chest when Mike took my hand and slowly pulled himself close to me. I could feel the tiny hairs on the back of my neck stand up as he slid his other hand into my hair. He held my jaw gently in place and guided my lips toward his. There was an explosion inside me when I felt his smooth lips touch mine.

After each movement of his mouth, a small breath escaped

his nose lightly and brushed against my skin. The smell of his cologne made me dizzy. It felt like we kissed for hours.

It was amazing.

When Mike finally pulled back, ending my very first kiss with easy, little kisses, he gave me a pleased smile. I said nothing. I felt comfort, and total peace. A feeling I hadn't experienced since my surgery began. Mike had given me the perfect gift. He gave me back a feeling of true happiness.

"Do you know the name of this song?" he asked, gesturing at the television.

As he stood up, the name of the band and the title of the song appeared in white block letters in the corner of the screen. "It's 'Big Empty,' by Stone Temple Pilots. It's the acoustic version," he told me. "You should get the CD."

"Okay."

"Cool."

And with that, he was gone. I heard him say good night to my parents and, moments later, I heard the limo door slam shut.

Some girls get their first high heels for their sixteenth birthday; others get a DJ at their party; and others may even get their first car. But I had the best gift of all.

I had Mike Gould.

And that made my sixteenth birthday very, very sweet.

# CHAPTER 10

# Duct Tape and All-Nighters

Me and Papa in our matching Christmas presents—we
both picked out a "writer" hat for the other
without even knowing it!

WHEN I WAS seven, I fell in love with a keyboard that my dad had
bought me for Christmas from the Fair. Music always held my attention, which thrilled my mom, who was anxious to support any
budding talent or interest I might have. So I began taking lessons
at a local piano teacher's very cluttered home. Today, I think his
place could probably be featured on one of those shows about
hoarders. I'd never seen a house with so much stuff. His music
room was positively chock-full, with sheet music, books, and potted plants covering nearly every inch of the space.

Somehow, I was able to concentrate among the clutter and I
quickly chose my favorite piece, one that I longed to play myself:
Beethoven's "Für Elise." It was quite a bold and ambitious choice
for a little girl. My instructor, impressed and maybe a little amused

that I had even heard of "Für Elise," agreed to help me learn to play it.

I climbed onto the piano bench—quite a feat in itself for someone just over three feet tall—and sat down beside him. My feet dangled high above the floor and the brass piano pedals. With his thumb and pointer finger he showed me the first four keys to the song. I picked up on it right away. I was excited and inspired to learn more. He played the next few notes. I repeated after him. And though they were the exact same notes that he had just played for me, something didn't sound right.

It was that beautiful echo created by the pedals as he pressed them down firmly with his feet. I couldn't reach them—not even close. And no matter how hard I tried to pull an echo sound out of the keys, when it was my turn to mimic what my teacher had played, my version was always different. It never sounded like it should. In time, I gave up and learned "Mary Had a Little Lamb" instead.

◆

I rang in 1997 with my mom and dad, nibbling on homemade chicken wings. I wasn't having a party or looking forward to a kiss when the ball dropped, but I was celebrating the length I had achieved in my legs thus far: a solid three inches. I was that much closer to whatever I wanted to reach.

But I was getting sick of my living room. I literally hadn't seen my own bedroom upstairs in over three months. I missed my pink lace curtains, my girly furniture, and my pile of stuffed animals. Despite the TV, stereo, and phone in the living room, I felt stuck. I needed a change of scenery. So Mom rented an adjustable orthopedic bed and set up camp for me back upstairs.

We put the new bed beside my big picture window. From

there, I could see the faint tip of Mount Wachusett crest above the trees, and Marlborough High School poke through the frozen branches across the street. I felt renewed. But still, I couldn't sleep soundly through the night. It was only a matter of time before my homeschooling began to suffer.

It was sleeting when I first met Richard, my tutor. At least, I thought that was his name. I was distracted by my clogged ears (another side effect of the pain meds) when he introduced himself. I was also struck by his brooding look and his slick black hair, doused in gel. He was in his twenties and seemed like he belonged in a coffee shop with his goatee, heavy tweed winter coat, and maroon scarf around his neck. Richard came prepared to work, but I don't think he was prepared for me.

I sat in the blue recliner and stared blankly out the window, still somewhere between sleep and the pain medicine lull. No matter how hard Richard worked, I could barely concentrate. High school algebra may as well have been quantum physics as I strained to focus on the equations he wrote out on the dry-erase board Mom had picked up from Walmart.

Our sessions lasted no longer than twenty-five minutes.

"Is it possible you can come later than seven thirty tomorrow?" Mom asked. "Tiffanie's medication takes the pain away for a while, but it doesn't make her comfortable enough to sleep solidly, so it would help if she got up a bit later."

"I can't," Richard said. "I have other appointments."

"All right. Tomorrow will be better," Mom assured him. "It will become easier with time." She hoped this would turn out to be true.

I hoped to wean myself off of the pain pills entirely but I needed relief. The skin around the wires in my feet was tearing with every inch I gained. The tendons and muscles in my calves grew tighter, making my skin look shiny and lacquered. My body was struggling to keep up. So Dad and I came up with one more MacGyver-esque fix for the skin ripping on my feet.

"Duct tape fixes everything," he told me, sticking pieces of tape to the tops of my feet and pulling my skin toward the wires to counteract the tearing. "There we go, how's that?" He rubbed the tape into place.

It brought me back to being a little girl the first time I'd gone through a lengthening procedure. With newly taped feet, I celebrated being well on my way to my fourth new inch.

Every day, right on time at seven thirty a.m., Richard returned, armed with euphemisms that drove me crazy. The poor guy didn't know what he had gotten himself into.

"This one has some meat on it," he said one morning, circling a difficult math equation with a red marker. My stomach churned at the thought of carcass scraps hanging off the edge of the whiteboard. "But this one," he said about a problem that was easier, "this one is *cake*."

In the kitchen, Mom was baking again and the sugary smell grew sickeningly sweet when it reached the living room. My stomach felt like it was turning somersaults around my Vicodin until, inevitably, the images of frosting-covered meat chunks pushed me over the edge.

I vomited in my chair.

With that, my lesson was done, and so was Richard.

Tom, my physical therapist, came nearly every afternoon during the week. Armed with folders and a range of motion-measuring devices, he also arrived with plenty of skepticism, criticism, and doubt.

"When are you going to stop lengthening?" he'd ask every day. The more my toes curled toward the ground as I turned my pins, the more nervous he became. "I think you've done enough," he'd say. "You should stop."

"It's fine, Tom," I replied every time. "They don't hurt. The more I move around with my walker, the more my toes will stretch in the opposite direction." At this point, I was slowly but surely approaching five inches. I felt excited and accomplished, and his words gnawed at my resolve.

I dealt with his concerned warnings as best I could, but it felt like Tom was directly challenging my future and my need for independence.

"You *can't* go much more," he'd say in a singsongy voice that infuriated me.

He loved to use one of the words I'd grown to hate. *Can't.* How could he tell me I can't do things, especially now? I had reached a big milestone! In any other situation, with any other doctor, my pins would have been long removed. But I was still lengthening. Tom didn't understand what it was like to be in my (orthopedic) shoes. He would never get the world I lived in or the hell I would suffer *without* the lengthening surgeries. How could he say he was there to help me progress if he didn't even try to understand me or where I was coming from?

One day, I snapped.

"They're toes, Tom, get over it!" I shouted, making him jump. "You're not my father; you're not even my friend! I will stop when I feel the need to stop. So please, just do your job and keep your opinions to yourself."

For a while, my little outburst had done its job, and that March, I had peace. But then the nagging began all over again, and Tom's fondness for the word "can't" returned.

"This isn't working," I said during one of our routine transfers from one chair to another.

"What's not working?" he asked, confused.

"You. I'm done."

Tom's cheeks grew red and his jaw dropped. He went into the kitchen and brought my mom back with him into the living room. Little did he know I'd been expressing my frustrations to her for weeks.

"Tell her what you just said," he ordered. I wanted to leap out of my chair and smack him across his smug face.

"I said that I'm done with your comments, I'm done with you insisting that I stop lengthening, and I'm done working with you," I replied as coolly as I could. I paid close attention to my mom as I spoke, praying she wouldn't surprise me and take his side. *Please, Mom,* I pleaded inside. *Please tell him that you agree with me.*

She said nothing, only moving toward the door and opening it. Tom gathered his things and left. Just like that. I mustered the remaining strength I had left, gripped my walker tightly with my hands, and moved myself from the couch into the blue recliner. My chest tingled from the exchange. I felt I had finally stuck up for myself and for what I wanted out of life. It was addictive.

"I'll call the home-therapy agency tomorrow," Mom said.

Trying to sleep at night soon became more and more difficult, and my attitude took a nosedive. I didn't have the patience to deal with anything or anyone. I was becoming less tolerant and tired of explaining myself. I had blinders on and saw nothing but my goal. Nothing else existed. I had even become less patient with my friends.

My friends would call sporadically to talk about the latest gossip and drama that filled the hallways of MHS. The last thing I wanted to hear about was who was having sex with whom, who was trying pot, or who was hosting the crazy Holiday Inn parties that I couldn't go to, but—"It would have been fun if you were there, Tiff!"

I couldn't relate to any of it, and I didn't want to.

"It makes you relax," a girlfriend told me about pot one night.

"So it's like Valium?" I asked halfheartedly while staring at my pin sites, wondering how bad it would be if I only cleaned them once a day instead of twice. They certainly *looked* clean.

"Like what?" my friend asked, as though I'd been speaking in a foreign language.

"Valium."

"What's that?"

"Never mind." The divide between me and my friends seemed to be getting bigger all the time. I had become an expert in pain meds. By my sixteenth birthday, I had been on Vicodin, methadone, morphine, OxyContin, Percocet, codeine, and fentanyl, and here was my friend, excitedly telling me how drugs helped her lose control. All I wanted was to get back in control.

What could my friends possibly be so desperate to escape from? To me, being pain-free for ten minutes was pure, unadulterated ecstasy, and I felt myself becoming bitter that they didn't appreciate the peace they had. My classmates didn't deserve their independence, because they took it for granted. No one in high school even deserved his or her body, I thought wildly. They *all* took the little things for granted. The ability to reach the combination lock on their lockers, the dollar slot in the soda machines, the sewing machine pedal in design class, and the ability to climb the bleachers—no one appreciated any of it. My classmates didn't have a clue what it was like not to be able to access these everyday things.

That winter, Dad carried me downstairs one morning after

Mom went to work. Groggily, I began my pin care routine in the
blue recliner. Going through the motions, I felt a cramp below my
stomach. It was a new sensation unrelated to my legs and I assumed it simply meant I had to use the bathroom. I called my dad
for help getting to the toilet. He lifted me out of the chair.

"You're bleeding," he said simply. I was confused. I hadn't
knocked my pins into anything, they weren't infected, and I
hadn't pushed myself too hard the day before. Where was the
blood coming from? In the bathroom, Dad helped me onto the
toilet. The blood was all over my shorts and stained the inside of
my thighs. Then it dawned on me: I'd just gotten my first period . . . with my *father* looking on.

Neither of us said a word. Dad stayed focused on helping to
clean me and change my clothes. There wasn't a single pad or
tampon in the house, so he improvised. He took a new roll of
toilet paper out from under the sink and unraveled half of it, creating a thick nest to line my underwear. If MacGyver were a father, he would have been proud.

As I adjusted my bulging, makeshift panty liner, Dad went
out into the living room to spot-clean the chair and layer it with
towels. Then he came back into the bathroom, scooped me up,
and deposited me back on the recliner like nothing had happened.

"There," he said as nonchalantly as possible. "You'll be fine
until Mom gets home. Just don't move."

I nodded, flipping through the TV channels, waiting until he
went outside before calling my mom. When Mom made it home
from her shift, she found me sitting in the blue recliner, still in my
toilet paper nest. With a package of maxi pads in hand, she burst
out laughing, apologized, and gave me a big hug as if to say, *It
could be worse.*

Judy Blume herself could not have prepared me for the way I welcomed my Aunt Flow.

That spring also signified the start of new things for me and Mike. For him, it was the beginning of his first serious relationship, with a girl from Westborough. The season was the beginning of a whole new world for me, too. That spring, I discovered the Internet.

One night, when Dad came home from work, he hoisted his massive Gateway 486 desktop PC monitor on top of my small hospital table.

"Take a look at this," he said happily. "It's better than television."

Back then, his desktop computer cost more than a thousand dollars and had only 32 megabytes of RAM. He set the clunky tower on a separate table next to my bed. All I needed to do was lean to my right, press the power button, and I could boot up. The machine purred, then toiled as Windows loaded. The screen glowed and the fans whirled inside. It was alive. And for once, my room was, too.

Each night, cast in the pasty glow of the screen, I settled into my orthopedic adjustable bed and found my own way to get out. The Internet became a place where I could communicate with—and relate to—so many people. Without having to move from my bed, I was connected to cyberspace. I became so consumed with my virtual travels that I discovered a much bigger relief—giving up my pain pills.

Unix systems, Linux, telnet, DOS, chat rooms, and BBSs (bulletin board systems)—I was into it all. Everyone online went by nicknames, or "handles." To decide on my own, I peered down at the monstrous contraptions attached to my legs and thought of the five-plus inches I had gained thus far. I decided to call myself "LiveWire."

I made new friends and though I didn't know them the way I knew the kids at school, I felt close to them. And I appreciated the fact that we didn't have to talk about drugs or alcohol. Instead, we chatted about real, interesting topics like Trojan horses, Bill Gates vs. Steve Jobs and Steve Wozniak, and the irrelevance of certain firewall security systems. We talked about things that distracted me from the pricking sensations tackling my legs. We shared our ideas about the battle for free information online and *The Hacker's Manifesto*, written by a hacker known only as the Mentor.

*And then it happened . . . a door opened to a world. . . . Rushing through the phone line like heroin through an addict's veins, an electronic pulse is sent out, a refuge from the day-to-day in competencies is sought . . . a board is found. This is it . . . this is where I belong. . . . I know everyone here . . . even if I've never met them, never talked to them, may never hear from them again . . . I know you all. . . .*

I had found a place to belong.

It wasn't long before I decided that I wanted revenge on the one person who had told me I *didn't* belong: Ms. Hart. And I was going to recruit for it. I posted a battle cry on the boards, and the response was nothing short of awesome. Many joined in with their take on what would be funny and "equally as mortifying" to do to her. Before I knew it, I had assembled a miniature army. Our battle plan included something we'd seen in the movie *Hackers*: listing her office phone number on shady sex sites (it was a little scary how easy it was to do that) and constructing advertisements that would humiliate her. Of course, there were ways around paying for these advertisements, too. In cyberspace, there were ways around everything.

One of my online friends spent time creating a program that would infect her office computer and cause the printer to go crazy.

Pages upon pages would be printed that read: "Ms. Hart is a diseased cow." I laughed at the image and fell asleep fantasizing about how embarrassed she'd be—even more than I had been.

None of this came together overnight, of course. First I needed her phone number, I needed to figure out what type of network MHS was running, and I needed a physical body to upload the virus into the system. This would require the help of someone at school. To my surprise, I found a good friend who agreed to do it—one who hated her computer class—and anything to get out of doing actual work sounded great to her. I had finally found a way to bridge the gap between my high school and me.

One of my online friends also suggested going beyond the boards and seeking out an elite hacking group. During one midnight conversation, I was directed to a Boston hacker organization. Excited and motivated, I wrote them an e-mail and told them my story. It was a while before I received a response, but when I did, two words jumped out at me right away.

*Sounds fun.*

But in the end, I found my hacker in Florida. In the mail, I received a square red disc with a message written on it in black marker. It read: "LiveWire, here is your disease." I had made a risky move, giving my home address to people I had never met, but I didn't care. Oblivious, Dad handed me the package, but Mom had grown very suspicious about what I was doing on the computer late at night and demanded to know what the disc was for. I refused to show her, fearful that if I put the disc into my dad's computer it would become infected. I couldn't think of a decent lie, either, so the truth came out.

Dad stood in the doorway with his evening rum and Coke during my admission. Tilting his glass and stifling a smile, he looked at me with what I could only interpret as an expression of approval.

"I like my martini shaken, not stirred," he said with a wink before leaving my room. Mom immediately threw out the disc and issued a singular warning.

"If you abuse the computer, you won't have a computer anymore."

I was stuck, and whether I liked it or not, she had the upper hand. I could not get to the computer on my own if she decided to take it away. I removed the programs that locked my dad out of his own PC and gave her my programming, operating system, and online security books that I'd picked up at the bookstore when we went to the mall. I even forfeited my personal notebook filled with IP numbers.

The game was officially over.

I never found out whether anyone actually made phone calls to Ms. Hart's office. It was frustrating to be left without answers, so I fantasized about what may have happened, hoping that Ms. Hart was embarrassed in the sports medicine room the way she embarrassed me. I wished my mom hadn't caught me, but I wasn't ashamed of what I'd done.

I turned my attention to catching up on sleep, exercising, and cleaning and turning my pins by day. I even found motivation to stay awake long enough to sit through an entire tutoring session with my new homeschool teacher, Sandy. I was hell-bent on graduating with my class.

"Do you have a fascination with meat or cake?" I asked her when she settled onto the couch with a stack of books and notepads during our first session.

"Um, no." Sandy stared at me, perplexed. Young and enthusiastic, she had a pleasant, casual way of speaking and reminded me of an older sister.

"Are you in pain right now?" she asked.

"No, I'm good. Now, what about the meat and cake?"

"I'm not sure what that has to do with your graduating on time," she said. Then it was Sandy's turn to question me. "If you're in pain, will you tell me so we can take a break? That's all I ask, that you're honest with me about how you're feeling." She smiled, studying my face. Sandy seemed to be unmoved by the sight of my pins. At least, she didn't let it disrupt our time together. I felt like she understood me.

By night, if I couldn't devise plans to embarrass Ms. Hart anymore, I decided I would write stories on the computer about humiliating her. There was so much I wanted to say to her but never did. Suddenly, I no longer felt confined. I had my own private world, free of the pain, prejudice, and ignorance I had come to know in reality. This was a wound that would not heal. I no longer cared to keep silent. My writing was my vengeance. So I stayed up late at night, writing a murder mystery involving the untimely passing of a high school teacher whose body was found in an ice machine, pounding away at my keyboard like the piano I never had.

Typing faster and faster with each minute that ticked past, I channeled Papa, mumbling, "That's good," at the end of a line that I particularly liked. I could barely maintain control of my fingers. It was as if I had an imaginary coach standing over my shoulder, dictating all of the experiences I had gone through and reminding me of the emotions attached to each one.

*Write! Tell the world!* I imagined him shouting as the words poured out of me. I was unstoppable, slamming down on the keys as if I were playing before a packed concert hall.

*Write! Write! Write!*

It was a rush that affected me more than any drug. I got a high off each sentence. The hairs on my arms stood tall as the paragraphs poured out on my screen. It even took away those persistent muscle spasms. Above all, it took away the painful memory of being humiliated in the sports medicine room.

That night, for the first time, time flew by. Minutes turned into hours. Before I knew it, the sun was coming up, and my father was getting ready for work.

Day after day, I began to find myself excited to do pin care at night, because it meant that, within the hour, it would be computer time. I forgot about taking pain pills altogether. They were out of the question, because I couldn't type or read the text on the screen when I was on them. I would cope with the pain, even throughout the grueling therapy, without the meds, because my new coping mechanism was writing. Despite being weighed down by rods and metal, I had finally found a way to be free.

# CHAPTER 11

# Victories

Graduating from Marlborough High.

SIX MONTHS INTO the bone-lengthening procedure with my shins, I woke up one April Saturday around noon. I cleaned my pins and craved a bowl of Blueberry Morning cereal. My formerly feeble appetite was back with a vengeance and it made my mom smile when I asked for seconds. After breakfast, I lifted my legs and swung them over the bed as I had done so many times before, gripped my walker, and began my long journey to the bathroom. It was an average Saturday morning.

At first.

I fixed my gaze on my feet as I slowly passed the blue recliner Dad had brought upstairs from the living room. Eventually I made my way through the door frame and into the hallway. Noticing that I was once again looking down as I walked, Mom yelled at me.

"Stop looking at your feet! Look in front of you!" It was just her helping me with my physical therapy now, and during times of frustration I called her "G.I. Jane." Standing up straight was the least of my concerns, but a major one of hers for the sake of the rehabilitation process. I had to relearn proper posture, but making it to the toilet on time was a much higher priority.

I wiggled and pushed my clunky walker through the narrow doorway. The wooden doorjamb was riddled with deep indentations from my many trips to the bathroom. As I neared the toilet, I lifted my eyes, maneuvering my body in that direction. Then I saw it. Out of the corner of my eye, I noticed something that literally stopped me in my tracks, bringing the wheels on the front of my walker screeching to a halt. In the mirror, I saw a girl—I took in her torso, then her shoulders, her neck and head. It took a moment to realize that girl was me.

It was the very first time I saw the reflection of my upper body in the mirror.

My shoulders looked so strong, I thought, as I stood gaping at my reflection for several moments. I had seen myself in full-length mirrors before, standing next to a friend of mine or passing by a fitting room at Macy's, but I had never seen the reflection of anything below my neck in my own bathroom mirror. It was as if I had switched places with someone else, swapped bodies somehow with someone taller. But it was *me*.

The pain I faced every day in my legs, the burning and the tight, stinging aches that crawled up and down my shins—it was worth it.

Then the craziest idea occurred to me—what would happen if I tried to turn on the water? Anxious, I lifted my walker and pivoted toward the sink. My walker smashed into the under-sink cabinet, denting the wood. I didn't care. I reached out and gripped the knob for hot water, then the cold, turning them on and off individually and then together.

Giggling to myself, I traced my fingers across the deep belly of the sink. I could reach it *all*. Everything! The blue Rubbermaid stool sat in the corner alone—I didn't need it anymore. The soap, the towel hanging above the rim of the sink, the plastic container stuffed with Q-tips—nothing was off-limits.

Then Mom's reflection appeared in the mirror behind mine. No words were exchanged. There was nothing we could say that would adequately express the joy we both felt at my discovery. It was like I had glitter pulsing through my veins, tickling my insides, and without warning it burst out of me. I laughed with such reckless abandon and glee that my mom couldn't help but join in, laughing hysterically until we were both wiping away tears.

I couldn't wait to call Mike, but when he answered, he sounded distracted, like he was somewhere else. I begged him to come over.

"You have to see this!" I shouted over the phone, gripping it tightly.

He promised to stop by.

My world had changed overnight, even though it had actually been six long months of turning pins, therapy, and struggle. That Saturday, I lost myself in the mania of my excitement and moved all around the house to see what else I could reach. Mike never did come over, but I hardly noticed in the excitement.

Light switches were next, and I found that I could turn them on and off with ease. Towels were within reach, too, and I could use them in both the bathroom and in the kitchen, or even fluff and fold them, draping them over the rods. No longer did I need them as lassos to extend my reach. I could now use towels the same way everyone else did—to dry my hands after washing them in the sink. Overjoyed, I hollered to my dad for him to carry me downstairs to see what else I could do. I made my way to the coffeemaker, where I found that I could grip the handle and pour a cup, but the buttons and the filter were all still a bit too high for me to reach. This would come later, I thought, as I gained more height. I still had my thighs to lengthen.

Before long, that time had come. In my bed one afternoon, I realized something was wrong. Each time I turned the L-wrench, it pushed back against me. It was as if my body were issuing a bold, loud warning.

Normally, turning my pins felt like nothing at all; the quarter-millimeter turn was too small to feel. But this time I felt a strange pressure in the center of my shin and the muscles on the bone felt tighter the more I tried. It became too painful to turn.

"Something's not right," I told my mom. "It's harder to turn."

"Does it hurt?" Mom looked concerned and then motioned toward the pins, asking if she could turn them. I nodded.

Slowly she pushed downward on the wrench and her eyebrows centered in the middle of her forehead. She felt it, too. She took out the wrench, set it on my lap, and looked at me.

"What do you think?"

"I think it's time to stop. Can I have the phone? I need to call Dr. Mortimer."

I was never so happy to go to UMass for surgery. It was time for the second phase of gaining my independence.

The battle plan: to remove the pins in my shins and, in the same operation, break, drill, and insert new fixators and stainless steel pins into my femurs.

Before I knew it, that surgery was completed and I was waking up with new pins in my thighs. The fog of anesthesia clouded my brain and I couldn't tell where one thought ended and another began. But I knew I was in the recovery room and I knew the recovery room nurse holding my hand was Kathy Sheridan. Her presence automatically calmed me and I felt safe from all the chemicals that took over my body. Instead of using a set of metal half-moons like the ones that had been around my shins, Dr. Mortimer had attached the same device to my thighs that Dr. Shapiro had used on my arms years before. A black bar, the thickness of a remote control, fixed along the outside of each of my thighs, anchored into the femurs.

"I feel heavy," I said to Kathy through dry lips. My throat felt coarse, as if I'd been screaming.

"How, honey?" she asked, guiding ginger ale to my mouth and helping me sip.

"I feel like . . . I'm stuck. Can't move."

She shifted the IV and heart monitor wires around me and adjusted the blankets. I hated being caught in wires.

"Still?" she asked.

"Yes. I'm stuck." I felt like my legs were being tugged deeper and deeper into something, but I didn't know what. I knew this sensation was real and it wasn't my imagination. I was definitely stuck.

Kathy gently pulled my blankets down and finally saw what I'd been feeling. The tips of my pins had embedded themselves into the mattress. My legs were truly stuck in the bed. That was the first sign that this phase of my bone lengthening would be entirely different from the last. I'd have to sleep on a tough nylon air bed now. Using my walker was also different. There wasn't enough room to move inside of it. The pins jutting out from my thighs hit the bars of the walker in all the wrong places. Crutches were the other option. This demanded a level of skill and balance that took me weeks to perfect.

"Now that you can move easier, you need to get outside. The weather is too beautiful," Mom insisted one sunny afternoon, afraid that I'd suffer from surgically imposed cabin fever.

The breeze felt nice as I stepped onto our farmer's porch. The flowers in Mom's garden were beginning to sprout. I wondered whether I'd grow faster than the roses.

Mom brought out some iced tea and helped me sit down and extend my legs out in front of me. Together, we watched several cars and the occasional truck enter our street and pull into a neighboring driveway. It was good to get out, even if it was only to sit in our front yard. Then I heard the garage door open and Dad pulled the Grand Prix out into the driveway for a good wash and waxing, a little ritual of his in the warmer months.

I watched him put the car in park, then get out and feed a green hose into an orange bucket. Soapy suds crested over the rim and spilled down to the pavement.

"I can't wait to wash my own car," I said between tiny sips of cold tea.

"Soon enough," Mom said.

"I can't wait to *drive* that car and get it dirty," I added with a laugh.

Mom didn't respond right away. She swiveled toward me, practically popping out of her seat.

"Why wait?"

Confused, I watched her stand up, take four big steps to the end of the porch, and lean over the railing.

"Gerry!" she shouted over the gushing water. "Gerry! Stop! Wait! Come up here for a second."

"Why?"

"Just come up here for a second, would ya?"

Reluctantly, he turned off the water and climbed the stairs up to the front door.

"*What?*"

Mom addressed us both. "Tiff, how would you like to try and reach the pedals now?"

"Reach the pedals of what?" Dad asked.

It was a crazy idea. But it was brilliant.

"Oh no. No, no, *no!*" Dad shook his head in disapproval. "You've got to be kidding me."

Mom ignored his protests and picked up my walker, rushing it over to the car. I outstretched my arms, ready to be picked up.

"You've lost your mind! You can't get in the car, c'mon!" Dad shouted.

*Hurry up and just grab me!* I thought, waving my arms at my mom.

"Robin!" Dad shouted.

"*Gerry!*" Mom mimicked.

"She can't get in the car—what if she breaks a leg?" He was getting more upset by the minute. But his question was pretty hilarious.

"Hello? Have we met? Broken legs, meet my dad. Dad, meet my already broken legs," I said with a snort. Mom let out a hearty laugh of her own.

Dad realized this was a battle he could not win. Reluctantly, he walked by my mom and scooped me up in his arms, carrying me to the car. Mom opened the door and I took in the scent of Armor All on the faux leather interior. The gray fabric of the seats felt warm from the sun beating down on them through the windshield. It was all just spectacular. I felt as if I had never been in a car before.

"Watch out," Mom said and she slammed the door. I had plenty of room to sit between the door and the center console while allowing extra room for my pins. I sat staring out the windshield and gripped the steering wheel, my breath shaky with excitement.

Mom sat down in the passenger seat and dangled her car keys in front of me. "Start it up."

It was more exhilarating than I ever could have imagined while watching those BMW commercials. I didn't waste any time—I jammed that sucker in as fast as I could and turned. The sound was like excitement personified.

"Can you reach the pedals?"

I hesitated, scared at the thought that maybe I couldn't reach. But I lifted my right leg anyway and hoped for the best. My foot just barely touched. "Not yet."

"That's all right. It will get there."

Week after week, Dad carried me down the cellar stairs to the Grand Prix. No longer did I just sit on the front porch daydreaming and sipping iced tea while staring at the roses. Instead, I turned the key to the ignition and felt the hum of my future down the road.

I measured my progress—one millimeter at a time—until the moment arrived: I could reach the pedals. The pulsating ache under my ankles was now a distant memory. I pushed a button to lower the windows and then let out a scream like none other.

"I did it!"

Mom rushed down the porch steps, my old Cyndi Lauper tape in hand. It was time to have fun. In the driveway I practiced three-point turns and fixing my mirrors. Then, with Cyndi blaring full bore out the windows, I took off down the driveway and down my street.

The excitement just kept coming in the days that followed. Shortly thereafter, I took a therapeutic soak in our hot tub in the cellar after a particularly grueling exercise session. I sat in the water, allowing it to relieve the tightness in my tired muscles. My legs felt buoyant and my body warm as I enjoyed the knocking massage of the jets on my muscles. My skin was numb from stretching the nerves near the surface, but the bubbles seemed to kick those same nerve endings into gear and my legs felt alive again.

I thought back to my driving adventure days earlier and wondered what would happen if I tried to cross my legs. It was such a simple, unconscious movement that I witnessed others do time and time again. And it was another small but significant move that I had long since accepted I would never be able to make.

Or could I?

As the foam churned around me, I lifted my right leg up and gently dropped it over my left. It worked. Laughing wildly, I yelled at the top of my lungs.

"Mom!"

She rushed into the cellar with her eyes wide, sighing dramatically when she saw that I was okay.

"You *have* to stop doing this," she said as sternly as she could through a smile. "I think there's something wrong when you scream like that!"

"Look!" I shouted, pointing into the water.

Mom tapped a button for the bubbles to cease and she peered into the water as the surface settled. "Oh my God!" she screamed.

"I know!"

"You're crossing your legs!"

"I know!"

"You couldn't do that before!" She had tears in her eyes.

"I know, *I know!*" I shouted, gesturing for the phone. "I have to call Mike! He has to know about this!"

He sounded tired and sapped of energy from the moment he picked up.

"Can you come over?" I asked. He told me he had just woken up.

"It's seven at night. Were you already sleeping?" I prodded.

"Long night," he replied.

"Are you all right?" I lost track of why I had originally called. Something was wrong with him and it worried me.

"Babes, you worry too much. I'll be over tomorrow. Promise. And congratulations."

It was a full week before Mike made good on that promise. I heard his pickup truck in our driveway. Then I heard him cut the engine and slam the door behind him and walk across the lawn, stopping below my bedroom.

"Babes!" he called up to my window, pelting it with mulch chips. "Open the garage!"

"No!"

He paused, shocked, before yelling back.

"Why the hell not?"

"I'm mad at you!"

"*Why?*"

"You missed some of the best moments of my life that I worked hard for!" I screamed from my bed. "And the worst thing is, you don't even care."

"I told you I'd come over."

"That was over a week ago!"

More mulch chips smacked against the glass. "I'm here now. I obviously care—open the garage!"

I gave in. I needed to see him. I missed him and couldn't deny it.

I clicked the garage door opener and waited excitedly for him to appear in my doorway. With the garage door still rolling shut, he appeared. I had positioned myself on the edge of the bed in shorts and a T-shirt, legs dangling over the side to reveal my progress. I was planning to walk over to the blue chair at the other end of the room with my walker to further show off, but the look on Mike's face stopped me. We'd been talking on the phone, but we hadn't seen each other in person since my sixteenth birthday party in my full-length dress. That was eight months ago.

The sight of me now was too much for him to handle. He'd changed a lot since my party, too: Mike had gotten his license and another new girlfriend, but he seemed to lose interest in his beloved dirt bikes and he decided he wasn't going to college right away. There were new changes all around, but my body wasn't a good one, as far as he was concerned.

"Why won't you look at me?" I asked, inching my way to the chair, lifting one heavy leg at a time and pushing my body forward.

His gaze was fixed on the floor. He wouldn't watch me walk.

"Can you cover your thighs?" he asked, still not looking away.

"Why?"

"I don't want to see this."

"See what?"

"*That.* You, struggling and everything. Cover them. Please?"

"*This* is what I wanted to show you, though. I can reach things now." I made sure to make my tone upbeat and light to show him I wasn't suffering. I wanted to show him the pain had mostly faded, replaced by feelings of independence and accomplishment.

"That's great. You're a real live girl now," he said, still refusing to look at my legs.

"What's with the attitude, Geppetto?"

"I wish you'd accept yourself for who you are."

"This surgery has nothing to do with accepting myself. It has to do with living my life."

"You were living your life."

"Oh my God! I feel like I'm arguing with my dad!"

"I don't want to argue. It's not why I came over."

"If you didn't want to see this, then why did you come over?" I demanded, fighting back tears. I wanted to do more than show him some examples of the independence I had gained. I wanted to share my goals with him, like attending the prom. And I wanted him to be my date.

He didn't let me get that far. He just hugged me, said, "I love you," and left.

*   ❖   *

As the holiday season of 1997 approached, I was a full fourteen inches taller. After the four inches I'd gained in my legs as a kid, I'd added another six inches in my shins on the second go-round, and four more inches in my thighs. At four feet, ten inches, I could reach just about everything in the house (and on my body). For about three months, the pins stayed in my thighs in order to allow the new bone to develop in the space I'd created. During this time, I took my SATs from the blue recliner—a first for the test proctor. "This has to be the most comfortable setting I've ever seen a student take the SATs," he told me. Clearly, he had no clue. During my sessions with Sandy, we perfected my college essays and applications.

Once the new bone had filled in, the surgery to remove the pins in my femurs went by in the blink of an eye. In the recovery room I felt weightless, almost like I was floating above my bed. The blankets fell over the sides of my legs and for the first time in years,

I could feel the scratchy fabric against the thin skin of my entire legs. As a souvenir, Errol handed me a hazardous materials bag filled with the stainless steel pins that had been inside my legs. I felt compelled to roll over on my side and sleep, to enjoy the sensation of dozing off in a position other than on my back. With an audible giggle, I rolled over and enjoyed the sweetest sleep in years. I did my best to ignore the fact that I felt a slight pop in my left leg.

On Christmas Day, while my family gathered in the kitchen and the living room, I asked to be excused to my bedroom. The pop in my left thigh had grown into a dull ache and then a hard throb that made me grit my teeth in pain. For days, despite the sharp, twisting sensations, I continued to push through it, do my leg lifts, and walk around the house with my crutches. But the sensation soon grew too excruciating to bear. I had to go to the hospital.

"Now?" Mom asked. This was so unlike me that it worried her.

"Right now."

Dad joined her in the doorway.

"Can you move?"

"No."

"Want me to pick you up and put you in the car?"

"No! Don't move my leg. Something's really wrong."

"That's it. I'm calling an ambulance," my mother said.

"An *ambulance?*" my father and I said in unison.

"You don't act like this for it not to be something serious. If something's wrong, we're not making it worse."

The paramedics arrived, and the fire department trailed behind them. It was such a spectacle that you would have thought I'd had a heart attack.

"I should have just gone in the car," I said, shifting my weight while they loaded me onto a stretcher.

One paramedic put up his hand and motioned for me to stop. "Let us do this," he said.

"I'm not dying," I replied. "My leg just hurts."

"It's for your own safety."

I threw my hands up, annoyed at the fuss, and gave in, allowing them to help me. It all felt so silly, given what I'd already been through. Soon, I was back at the hospital under an X-ray machine when Errol flew through the door.

"Do you want some pain medication?" His tone was so urgent that I'm sure if I had asked for a bottle of scotch, he would have complied.

"No," I said slowly, puzzled. "I'm fine."

"Are you sure you don't want *anything*?" he asked again, his eyes practically bulging out of his head.

"No, I'm good. What's going on?"

"Well," he began, scurrying around the room, "we need to get you into surgery as soon as possible."

"What? Why?"

He clipped my X-ray onto the light board and flipped a switch. The bright fluorescent light cast a creepy glow in the radiology room. He pointed at a spot on the picture.

"Because of *this*."

I stared at the image of my femur. My thigh bone, the strongest one in the whole human body, had literally snapped in half. It now resembled a broken letter V turned awkwardly on its side.

Several hours later, I woke up covered in a thick, hard plaster. One leg was free, but my right leg and both of my hips were trapped. There was a hole cut out around my stomach so I could breathe without restriction, but I felt hot and itchy all over. I was in a body cast. There was no other way to stabilize my severely broken femur, Errol would later tell me. I looked at the clock on the wall in the recovery room and then it dawned on me. I had only months until graduation. As I watched the second hand circle the clock, I began to feel panicked about the time slipping away. How on earth would I walk across the stage at graduation now?

At home the next day, I was in bed on my back.

Again.

I asked Mom to strap a sand weight around my left ankle in order to keep up on the exercises as best I could. I lifted my left leg high in the air. While watching TV, I used an elastic resistance band to build up the muscles in my arms and I continued to eat chocolate Power Bars to keep up my strength. While Sandy went over corrections on my English exams, I clenched the muscles inside my cast and held them for five counts of ten. I did this every day for three or four months until, finally, it was time to get the body cast sawed off.

While I was home with my tutor, a reporter visited my assistant principal, Mr. Kamataris, at Marlborough High. He was covering a story about a rising star athlete at MHS, but ended up learning about me in the process. So he decided to do a story about me, too. A few days after the article about my surgeries (and my goal to walk at graduation) ran in our local paper, the cards started rolling in. Dozens of people I'd never met before were reaching out to wish me good luck and offered their prayers. I read each one with tears welled in my eyes. The support from total strangers was yet another nudge to keep going toward my goal.

Then one day, tucked inside a white envelope, arrived the biggest push of all: my acceptance letter to the University of Massachusetts Dartmouth. I was going to be a college girl! But first I had a graduation to walk in and that meant making up for lost time doing physical therapy, starting with the stepper in my room.

The machine was an eyesore, hulking over me and taking up way too much space in my room. Working out on the stepper was the most difficult exercise in my entire repertoire, but it was among the most important as well. If I could conquer the stepper, I could build my strength and stamina and—ultimately—walk longer distances in less time and in less pain. At first, I wasn't up for the challenge. I covered the machine with a towel and pretended it didn't exist. But it continued to taunt me, so I asked my dad to move it deep into a corner. That didn't work for long. I was literally in countdown mode for graduation and time was running out.

I had no choice—I had to confront the stepper. I pulled myself up onto the pedals and gripped the handlebars. I'll do three steps, I thought, and just see how it goes. On my first attempt, I could barely push the pedals down and complete a single step. From the tops of my feet to the backs of my thighs, my lower body screamed with pain, and I was quickly out of breath. I was frustrated, but the feeling of being defeated by an inanimate object made my motivation stronger.

"Dad!" I hollered after my first attempt on the stepper. He walked down the hall to my room. "Can you move this next to my bed?"

Dad looked confused. "It will be in your way."

"Exactly," I replied with a smile.

Every day, literally unable to avoid it, I stepped onto the machine. The tight, sharp pain began at my ankles again, crawled over my feet, and spread up my shins and thighs. Before long, it took over my hips. My goal was to stay on the stepper for the duration of an entire song.

The first three days I lasted no more than than thirty seconds. By the end of my first week I had made it to a minute, but I stumbled off of the machine and fell. I could barely move. As I lay limp on the floor with my face pressed into the rug, I thought about how little time I had left and I started to cry. I had reached my breaking point. If I couldn't walk at graduation, I would let everyone down, from my parents and friends to Errol to those who prayed for me and, most important, myself.

"This energy for crying could be used on the machine, you know," Mom said from the doorway. She reached a hand toward me and helped me to my feet. I wiped my eyes and sat down on the bed. "Thanks, Mr. Miyagi," I cracked. "I'll remember that."

"Hey, don't get mad at me. Get angry with yourself for giving up."

"Who said I was giving up?"

"You're on your bed crying. Looks like you've given up to me."

Her calmness infuriated me. "I'm in pain!" I shouted. "I'm allowed to cry when I'm in pain. I'm allowed to have one damn moment of weakness! You think this is easy? It's *not*, Mom! It hurts and I'm so tired of it. Exercising is all I do and I'll never be able to stop. I'll have to work hard to keep my body functional for my *entire* life!"

Silently, she left my room. A moment later, she returned with a straw, still in its wrapper, and a cup filled with pepperoncinis.

"Since you won't take pain pills, eat these peppers to help boost your adrenaline," she said. "And if the peppers don't help with the pain, use the straw to *suck it up* and get back on that stepper."

I had a long hard road out of hell and while I hated to admit it, Mom was right. Crying wouldn't help. It would only distract from my ultimate goal, and I needed to make good on what I told Errol when we first met. I *could* handle this pain. Each day from then on out, I stepped up to the machine, my mouth burning from the peppers, and turned on my music. I kept the straw Mom gave me on my bedside table as I reminder that the big day was approaching fast.

In the final week before graduation, I blasted through my goal of stepping for a whole song, and pushed myself through extended remixes. Mom would pass my door while making calls to plan my graduation party, flashing a thumbs-up as she walked by. I was so ready to walk across the stage and grab hold of my diploma—and my new life.

Graduation day was hot and breezy and I wore my school-issued white cap and gown. Once we arrived at school, I noticed that nearly everyone had puffy paint designs on their caps. I did not. They had symbols and quotes from the school clubs they belonged to and sports they played—memories of time spent in high school. I had nothing. I should have taped a few pins to my cap or *something*, I thought as I watched my decorated classmates crossing the stage. Then it was my turn. I stood up, forgot about my plain white cap, and slowly walked to the middle of the aisle in the auditorium. Screams and cheers erupted from the bleachers and I felt myself blush.

I hoped Mike was in the crowd like he promised. I knew Dr. Mortimer was there with his wife, Lorraine, and their kids, Daniel and Sophie. My uncles and aunts were there, and I was sure my mom and dad were standing up cheering. I looked at the rows of students who'd already walked and three boys I knew stood up and clapped. After them, the entire row came to their feet. Then, like a wave beginning at a baseball game, the entire section stood, clapped, and cheered me on. I watched them for as long as I could until I had tears in my eyes and the whole scene was just a loud, roaring blur. I had to move slowly, one foot in front of the other, down the lengthy aisle. It took me much longer than the other graduates, who easily breezed across the stage for their diplomas. I began to worry that I was taking too long, but the crowd's reaction reassured me.

I had a standing ovation.

Their cheers made me feel like I was ten feet tall as the principal came down off the stage and greeted me at the end of the aisle. Steadily, I reached out my hand, gripping my crutch with the other, and took my diploma. I had accomplished my goal and walked at my graduation. I won.

The moment I got home, I called Mike. His voice was groggy and soft and I immediately knew he'd been sleeping—he was doing even more of that these days—and had never come to watch me walk. I was furious.

"Where *were* you?" I shouted, my eyes filling with hot, angry tears. "You said you were coming—you promised! I *walked*, Mike. I actually walked to get my diploma and you missed it!"

"Oh, sorry. What time is it?"

I was stunned. What did he mean, *what time is it?* First he didn't go to prom with me, and now he'd missed the most important moment in my life?

"I'll be over for your graduation party," he said distractedly. His promise had no life behind it and the words died in the air between us. "I'm coming. Give me a half hour, babes. Love you."

Mike never showed up.

I didn't know what hurt worse, my tired, shaky muscles as I stood in the kitchen, or my heart.

# CHAPTER 12

# College Girl

The "after" picture! With Mom after my surgeries
were completed, at the same spot in the kitchen
where she'd taken my "before" photos.

THE UNIVERSITY OF Massachusetts campus in North Dartmouth
looked like a futuristic concrete maze. The tops of all the buildings were flat, and rumor had it that the architect had envisioned
flying cars being able to land on them by the twenty-first century.
In 1999, my mom and I drove down to the campus, which was
surrounded by the appropriately named Ring Road.

We arrived on a rainy day. The classroom buildings and dorms
looked damp, dreary, and uninviting—not at all what I'd been

picturing. I had everything I would need for the next nine months packed tightly into Mom's red Jeep Grand Cherokee (she had given me the Pontiac): new bedding, a shower caddy, pictures of me and Mike, canned food, a mini microwave, a few dishes, and lots of my favorite outfits. I drove close behind her through campus toward my dorm.

The rooms in my dorm building were small, and mine—a single amid mostly doubles—was even smaller. The furniture that came with it reminded me of the sickly chairs at Children's Hospital. A bed, desk, and bureau were crammed against one of the light blue concrete walls, and the rug was thin and brown, like the underside of a soggy pizza slice. As we stood in the doorway, Mom dropped my bags on the floor of the room. My room. I instantly felt homesick.

"We can make this work," Mom said, just as she had in our base housing in Texas with the scorpion.

Mom assured me that I'd feel better about living by myself as the days went by. But I didn't. With the first few days of college behind me, each night alone was still scary. I slept with the TV on, and I had the regular blaring of Limp Bizkit CDs from a nearby dorm room to keep me company, too. I lay awake in bed, reminding myself of what had led me to be here, alone, in a room and at a place that felt like an alternate reality. A part of me felt like I had made a big mistake. Maybe my dad was right and I had started college too soon. Maybe I should have waited, given myself a year, at least, to adjust.

But adjust to what? Up until this point, I had never been on my own, not for a week, or even a few days. The concept of independence was, for most of my life, a fantasy that played out in my imagination while sitting in the gut of my blue reclining chair. The reality was this: I had no idea how big the world really was or, more important, how I was going to fit into it.

I may have been scared to be a college girl, but back home in Marlborough, my dad was terrified.

Every night for two weeks straight, he made his way to my bedroom, flicked on the ceiling light, stayed in there for a few moments, and then walked out without saying a word to my mom. Finally, he broke his silence.

"How could you let her go? She's not ready."

"I didn't let her do anything," Mom responded. "She chose to go. If she's not ready, she'll tell me. She knows I'm only a phone call away."

But I never did make that phone call. Nor did I ever consider leaving, even as I watched dozens of students succumb to the pressures of freshman year and depart just as quickly as they arrived. I never viewed that as an option for me.

Every Monday through Friday, I'd force myself to get up, make my way outside, and wander through the winding trilevel corridors of UMass to find my classes. I walked in late to every class and my frustration and embarrassment made me feel so much smaller than my proud new height of four foot ten. Everyone whooshed by me confidently, holding their coffees, books, and notepads, like they knew what they were doing and where they were going, at all times. In my fantasy while undergoing the bone lengthening, I was that girl walking the hallways with a purpose and a smile.

But the truth was, I had no clue. I wasn't that girl I had dreamed of at all. The surgery didn't change these aspects of my life as I had naively thought it would. I knew no one at school. With each week that passed, I ached to go back home to the familiarity of my room and even the blue reclining chair. The world beyond my house moved so much faster than I had ever considered.

And I hated it.

Every Thursday, or "Thirsty Thursday," as I learned that they were called, the girls in my hall would gather with their doors open and music blasting. As they got ready for a night of partying at the Dell, where the upperclassmen lived, a thick cloud of hairspray and perfume would fill the halls, clashing with the aroma of my Salisbury steak microwave dinner that I ate alone in my room.

Early in the new morning, usually around two o'clock, they'd return stumbling, laughing, and yelling. I always hesitated to go out into the hallway during these times of madness, but our shared bathroom was at the other end of the hall. One Thursday night, I bravely made my way down there.

"Hello?" A voice called out from the handicapped stall. Her stilettos were kicked off and poking out beneath the door. She reeked of smoke, sweat, and vodka.

I tiptoed into the second stall, moving as quietly as I could, but I gave myself away coughing once I got a whiff of the sour air trapped in the bathroom.

"Helloooo?" she drawled again. "Who's in here?"

"Tiffanie," I said, standing perfectly still. I felt awkward and nervous, and I just wanted to use the bathroom in peace.

"Tiffanie who?"

"I live down the hall," I told her.

"Tiffanie? Tiffanie. Oh my God. Why don't I know you? Do I know you?" she slurred. I wondered whether I sounded that way when I was doped up in the hospital.

"I don't think so," I answered.

"Were you at the Dell tonight?" she asked, topping off each word with a drunken trill.

"No," I said and then quickly decided against going to the bathroom.

I pushed open the door and, in a rush to get back to my room, smacked into two guys stumbling down the hallway. They were clutching red Solo cups, their beer sloshing over the rims as they staggered along, looking lost.

"Sorry!" one shouted over his shoulder. The other one just looked confused.

I was embarrassed, said nothing, and walked as quickly as I could to my room, where I immediately closed and locked the door. No one knew who I was—the drunk girl in the bathroom confirmed that beyond a shadow of a doubt. To drown out the fears that I had made a costly mistake by going to college too soon, I turned my TV on and let a *Fresh Prince of Bel-Air* rerun distract me. The channel selection was minimal—UMass Dartmouth had yet to negotiate a cable deal for its students. But anything was better than my racing mind and the thumping and squealing I could hear through the walls. I was forced to listen to my neighbor having sex.

Then I had a new worry: *What if I never get to experience that myself? What if I'm never seen by others as someone to date?* Clearly I didn't fit in with the other college students so far. Would I ever be loved that way? It was too much to ponder at such a late hour, so I tried my best to ignore the sounds, but I couldn't ignore what I was feeling: I wanted to go home.

I was also struggling in my classes, not to mention just getting to them. While other girls whizzed by me holding their lattes and purses, my wooden crutches rubbed my armpits raw. I avoided wearing short-sleeve shirts and tank tops, fearing someone would notice the crimson rash. No matter how warm it may have been, I always wore long-sleeved shirts or sweaters.

I ate alone every night in my room while everyone else went to dinner in pairs and packs. Some of the girls in my dorm walked past my door hand in hand with their dates. I fantasized about where they were going. The Olive Garden? The 99 Pub down the road? Maybe they were heading somewhere fancy in Providence, a restaurant adorned with twinkly lights, votive candles, and white tablecloths. More than anything, though, I wondered if I'd ever have a boyfriend of my own.

When the first semester of my freshman year was over, I couldn't have been happier than to return to Marlborough. Before Christmas, Mike came by to see how my freshman year was going. There were no wood chips and no yelling this time. Instead, I met him at the front door.

"Hey, what's up?" he asked. Always a rhetorical question and never one I really needed to answer. A hug did just fine.

He brought a card for me with a written invitation to dinner inside. I was tempted to ask for him to honor it by walking me down the hallway of my dorm, holding my hand. I watched him tuck the card beside some funny newspaper clippings Papa had given me to post on the corkboard in my dorm room. For the moment, things between Mike and me seemed back to the way they were supposed to be. We had long forgotten our fight.

"Babes, you're actually kind of hot now," Mike said with a wink. "But don't let it go to your head. I'm proud of you."

I felt myself blush a bit and I thanked him quickly before delving into how tough college had been for me. It was all so wild, I told him, and nothing like I'd expected.

"Wild how?" he asked, a mocking edge in his voice.

"I hear people having sex constantly."

"So?"

"*So?* It's horrible!"

"Sex isn't horrible."

I snorted in reply.

"Do you think you'll ever have sex?" Mike continued.

"I don't know," I replied, slightly annoyed and embarrassed.

"Well, you thought of everything else you want to do in life. Have you thought about having sex?"

"Of course I've thought about it."

"How have you pictured your first time?"

I fell silent as I considered for a few moments whether I could share something so personal with Mike. Then I caved.

"I picture slow music, candles, and pink roses everywhere. I picture wearing something cute with sparkles or ruffles and bows. And I picture a smile on his face, whoever he may be, and falling asleep next to him as he holds me tight and safe in his arms."

Mike sighed. "See, that's the problem with you girls. You aim way too high and you want the knight in shining armor in the movies. Then you get disappointed when it doesn't happen."

"Anyway!" I said, eager to change the subject, "I have too much to do first, like get off these crutches. There's no use talking about dreaming about a knight."

"Having crutches doesn't prevent you from having sex. But if you are going to hang on to your little fantasy, you may want to ditch those sweaters you wear all the time," he teased. "You're going to have to show your scars."

"All that aside, everything at college is just different and scary," I said dismissively.

"Of course you're scared; you're finally on your own," Mike said. His voice was soothing and I began to feel silly for being so uptight. "You haven't even crossed the street by yourself and now you're miles and miles away."

"What are you talking about? I've crossed the street."

"Oh yeah? When?"

"In the past."

"Babes, you have never crossed the street in your life. Admit it."

I paused and thought for a moment.

"Admit it," he urged again.

I thought back to all that time with the pins, and living in Texas and Douglas, but literally couldn't recall a single road I had crossed on my own. Once again, even though it pained me to admit it, Mike was right.

And he knew it.

"I'm right!" he exclaimed. "I'm right! See! Listen to me, babes. You're just catching up on the little shit others have always done and don't pay attention to anymore. The big stuff is going to scare the crap out of you if you let it. So don't let it."

"How do I do that?"

"I don't know," he said, standing up to give me a hug. He was making the visiting rounds with everyone home from college, I figured. So many people wanted Mike's attention. I wished for more time with him, just like I always did.

I followed him to the door and pressed him for an answer.

"But, Mike, *how* do I stop being so scared?"

He walked down the porch steps and paused, flashing that brilliant smile. Then he gestured to the road down the hill, illuminated by only a sliver of light from a lone streetlamp.

"I don't know . . . try crossing the street?"

While I stood shivering on the porch, Mike jogged back to his truck, climbed inside, and smacked the horn twice before driving down the road and out of sight.

After the holidays, I returned to UMass and stared out the window of my dorm room, watching crowds of people cross Ring Road. The snow was packed into a thin layer across the sidewalks. If I was to take Mike's advice, I decided it would have to wait until the spring.

That winter, Thirsty Thursdays returned and so did the squeaking beds. As if to make up for lost time during the holiday break, couples stumbled into dorm rooms even more frequently, without regard for anyone who might be trying to sleep or study. I dug into my messy desk drawer and pulled out a set of headphones. Then, over the music playing on my laptop, I heard shouting. Pushing the headphones off my ears, I listened to the cries coming from just beyond my door.

"He promised!" cried a female voice. "He *promised* me!"

I opened my door and found one of my hallmates sitting on the floor in a corner with her back against the wall. Her face was red and streaked with tears.

"He promised he would be right back," she continued, looking up at me. "He said he would stay the night with me this time."

I said nothing, just moved closer to her to listen. I'd never felt such empathy for a stranger before. She continued to cry as she told me about what a disaster her date had been. In my fantasies about having a boyfriend, being lied to or deceived never crossed my mind.

"I'm Crystal, by the way," she said with a sniffle. "That's my roommate, Larissa." Crystal motioned to the open door. Standing in the door frame, in Tweety Bird slippers, Larissa smiled and then joined us on the floor. It was nearly six months into my freshman year and I had finally begun to befriend my hallmates.

Though I had started to become more comfortable, college still wasn't what I was hoping it would be. So I spent many a weekend back home in Marlborough. On Fridays, Dad would pick me up in his big red truck, blasting the Beatles, and bring me home for the weekend, only to do the reverse early Monday morning before my classes began. By shortening the time that I stayed in my dorm room (which was now fully adorned in clippings and comics Papa gave me when I went home), the end of the school year arrived quickly and I told myself that my sophomore year would be better.

At home that summer, I fell back into my old habit of sleeping in until the early afternoon hours. So when the sharp ring of the house phone tore through one peaceful morning, it was awfully jarring. I'd only gone to sleep a few hours earlier. The sound jolted me awake and I knocked the receiver off the base to silence it.

"Tiffanie?" a little voice said before I had a chance to say hello.

"Hey," I replied sleepily. It was my cousin Gina. We hadn't talked in years, and she *never* called me. I felt my pulse pounding in my temples out of aggravation.

"I just wanted to see how you are . . . how are you?"

"I'm tired," I replied, squinting at my bedside clock. It was a little after eight a.m.

"I'm so sorry," she said, her voice cracking as she sniffled.

"Wait, how are *you?*" I asked, concerned and suddenly wide awake.

"I'm all right, I'll be fine. I just know you were so close. I'm so sorry."

"Gina," I began slowly, "what are you talking about? It's early. Is everything okay?"

She paused and inhaled sharply.

"You . . . you don't know?"

"Know *what?* What are you talking about?"

Gina burst into tears.

"It's Mike."

"What about him?" I interrupted, confused and annoyed.

Gina sobbed and didn't say anything.

"Gina! What about him?" I demanded.

"I work at the hospital and I was told that a girl is coming in for treatment, because she found a guy named Mike Gould. She found him."

"Found him where?"

"He committed suicide over the weekend, Tiffanie. He hung himself."

And then I went deaf. My stomach contracted and a nauseating ripple crawled up my throat. Gina was making no sense at all. Mike was fine. I had spoken with him a few days earlier and he'd made no mention of anything wrong. He would have told me.

It felt like the room was closing in around me, and I couldn't hold the phone anymore. It was too heavy and I could hardly breathe.

I tried to get out of bed but I got tangled up in the sheets and went crashing to the floor. The phone quickly followed, landing next to me. Gradually my hearing came back, and I heard a vicious scream grow louder and louder until it filled the room, the hallway, and then the whole house. Mom bolted out of her room and flew down the hall.

"Where are you? How did you fall?" she shouted in a panic. She looked down the stairs, expecting to see me at the bottom before realizing I was in my bedroom. "Who's on the phone? Why are you screaming?" She dropped down on her knees and squeezed my shoulders, searching my face for an answer.

I couldn't bring myself to tell her what had happened. I just kept wailing, in more pain than I'd ever felt. Mom grabbed the phone, and Gina told her what had happened while I tried to process the idea that I'd never see Mike again.

The remaining days of that summer were a total blur. All I did was watch television and bicker with my mom. One minute I'd feel infuriated with Mike. I'd curse at him and fling my hateful

words into the air, calling him selfish, weak, and a roaring hypo-
crite.

"How dare you give up on life entirely when you never let me
give up!" I'd scream at no one in particular. "You were perfect.
You had everything and everyone! You would not allow me to
ever, ever feel bad for myself, but what about you? Why didn't you
ever reach out to me? I was always there if you needed me; all you
had to do was say something! Anything!"

I hated him for what he did, but I loved, missed, and needed
him so much more.

Then the next hour would strike, and the roller coaster of
emotion would scream downhill once again. I'd cry, wail, and beg
for it just to be a terrible, horrible nightmare. I tried to piece together how Mike could have done such a thing. It was like trying
to put together a thousand jagged puzzle pieces that refused to fit
one another. I dissected our conversations a hundred times over
in my mind. Mike had told me that he was selling his truck and
buying a Mustang instead. That struck me as odd. He loved his
truck, but I didn't question him. Now I wished more than anything that I had.

In a way, I didn't want to understand why he took his own life.
I was angry and I didn't think I could forgive him. And then the
cycle would begin again, and the anger would erupt once more.

When my attempt to distract myself with mindless television
failed, I returned to the one thing that never let me down—
writing.

As I wrote, the hours melted away, much as they had when I
was turning my pins. I wrote and wrote, and I'd shut down the PC
only to turn it back on as soon as I awoke and then I'd write some
more. Dad would get up for work at four a.m. and walk by my
room to see that I was still awake, still writing.

A few weeks later, the wind blew gently through my hair as I stood, gripping my crutches tightly, on the perfectly manicured lawn of the Northborough cemetery. Some loose strands from my ponytail tickled my nose as I gazed down at Mike's dark gray tombstone and an eternity candle that was burning softly next to it. Someone had placed his dirt bike racing number, 107, against the tombstone, along with tiny toy dirt bikes arranged atop the mulch at the base of his resting spot.

I hadn't gone to Mike's funeral. I couldn't bring myself to say good-bye that way. But now, standing at his grave, I began to accept that Mike would no longer call me. Never again would I hear his adorable lisp or those wood chips tapping against my window. I also found a way to accept that everyone has troubles in life and Mike was hurting. And for whatever reason, he didn't want me to know. Maybe I had been the selfish one, because for years it was all about my surgery. I never asked him if he was all right.

I had printed out the lyrics to "Wonderwall," which I always thought of as our song. Below them, I wrote: *I love you. —Babes.* Slowly I leaned forward, rested it beside the tiny toy bikes, and let myself cry. And I promised Mike, out loud, that I would live the life I fought for and nearly forgot to appreciate. That meant going back to UMass in the fall. I'd even cross my first street.

⚫━◆━⚫

Huge cement flowerpots lined the UMass parking lot. They were heavy structures in place for security reasons, but until now I had managed not to drive into them as I backed out of my parking space after my English class. I had specifically planned my sophomore year schedule around every writing, literature, playwriting, and screenwriting class I could find.

As much as I loved the Grand Prix, and as good as it felt to be behind the wheel, there were large blind spots I always had trouble working around. If that car was filled up with water, I was certain I could do laps from the front seat to the back. It was a tank.

Back at my dorm, I called my mom to tell her what had happened. She said she expected a fender bender at some point and my dad, in the background, assured me with a shout, "It's nothing that can't be fixed!"

I smiled at the thought that I had just gotten into my first fender bender. Just like everyone else. My bumper now proudly displayed a sign that I had experienced a benchmark screwup like so many other kids my age.

Just as I hung up the phone, my door flew open.

"Tiffanie!" Larissa shouted. "What happened to your car?" The concern in her voice beckoned other hallmates, who all gathered in my room.

"I hit something, I guess." I laughed it off.

"Oh my God! I'm glad you're okay. Are you going home this weekend to get it fixed?"

"I'm not sure."

"Girl, you can't leave it busted like that. You gotta do something."

Then I had an idea.

"Maybe it's time I look into getting a new car."

Back home while on break, my parents had given me a chore. It was kind of a ridiculous notion for someone my age to have chores for the first time, but I had never been physically able before. Now my job was taking out the trash. Even more ridiculous? I *loved* doing it. I was finally tall enough to stand over the bin, grip the elastic band, and lift it out. The sound the can made as it fell away from the bag was music to my ears.

"You ready?" Mom asked. We had a shopping trip like none other ahead of us. I tied the red strings of the bag and handed it to her to bring with us out to the driveway.

After a familiar drive down the highway toward Worcester, we were pulling into the Shrewsbury BMW parking lot. My mom supported my longtime dream to drive the car that had inspired me, outlandish as it may have been, and now we were here. We sold the Grand Prix and used the money for a down payment on my would-be new car. Mom was determined to show me a way to make my dream a reality.

We walked into the showroom together and I felt like I was living out a fantasy. Immediately I zeroed in on *the* car—my car—that I had only seen flashing by on commercials for years, never up close. It was even more magnificent than I thought. The Z3 was perfect, it was gorgeous, and it practically grinned at me on the showroom floor.

"Would you like to sit inside?" asked a salesman. He opened the door and I handed my crutches to my mom, lowering myself down into the driver's seat.

The roadster sat low to the ground, and the bucket seats hugged my body. The fresh new leather smell was intoxicating. I gripped the steering wheel and imagined whizzing by my house and back to school.

Everything was compact inside—it was the perfect fit. I stretched my leg out to feel the surface of the pedal under my foot. Part of me hesitated, fearful I wouldn't be able to reach, but I was pleasantly surprised when, with a simple adjustment of the driver's seat, the ball of my foot easily met the gas pedal. My dream had come true, and I had accomplished exactly what I had imagined. The car was mine.

When I drove the roadster to school, my friends were always

excited to join me for a ride. If anyone needed hairspray, mascara, or beer, I made sure to volunteer, just to have the chance to drive. But the biggest thrill in my new car came in a most unlikely place: the drive-through Wendy's just off campus.

One day, after ordering a junior bacon cheeseburger and a Coke at the outdoor speaker (a place I'd never seen from the driver's side), I did something I only dreamed would one day be possible: I drove around to the pick-up window and easily reached outside to pay for my food. Finally, after so many years of fantasizing about such little exercises in independence, I was *doing* them.

◆

Under a cold, moonlit sky that winter, I stood in front of the apartments at the Dell. I couldn't believe I was there. Somehow, I had mustered up the gumption to rush Phi Sigma Sigma, and I was about to go to my first sorority party.

I had found their flyer a week before deciding to rush. The theme of this week's party was *Charlie's Angels* and I considered it to be a sign. I had come to think of Mike as my angel because, through his death, I finally learned to truly live my life. Plus, joining a sorority seemed like a great way to get involved and meet people. Phi Sig, as I would come to know it, was nothing like the stereotypes I'd heard about sororities. For starters, it wasn't made up of only tall, thin, Barbie-doll types. Phi Sig welcomed girls of all shapes and sizes. The sisters were from all different races and backgrounds, and some were tall and skinny while others were short and round. They were inclusive, funny, and warm. And it was clear to me, even as an outsider, that they all had one thing in common: how much they genuinely enjoyed being there. It seemed like they appreciated the little things in life, too (even if that didn't include taking out the trash or flipping on a light switch), so I could certainly relate.

Their motto was "Aim high." When I hung out with the Phi Sig girls, I didn't feel like I had to fit into any particular mold. I could just be myself, and they seemed to really like me.

In my first interactions with the Phi Sig ladies, I wondered if they did those girly group things. Did they gather in one girl's room at night to watch movies and order in pizza? Meet between classes to gossip? Borrow each other's hairspray? I had never done any of those things and wanted so desperately to be able to say I had. Maybe this was my chance.

One of the Phi Sig sisters, Nicole, was average height and on the voluptuous side and she embraced everything about what made her different. Her commanding presence and lack of filter when she talked made her stand out—she spoke my language. She made being different (and being loud!) seem fun, and it felt natural to be by her side, as if I were her apprentice.

So it was only natural that when it came time to assign the new girls "big sisters," she would be mine. With me as her "little," Nicole invited me to that party at the Dell. So this was what the girls in my hall experienced the first few weeks after enrolling at UMass? I thought to myself when I arrived. *This* was the thrill of being at the Dell at night, to be part of the organized chaos of drinking and partying that seemed to come so naturally to everyone? I tried to pretend it was natural for me, too.

I took it all in and watched the partygoers outside before I worked up the nerve to enter through the apartment door to meet up with Nicole. It was intoxicating to be around so many happy, laughing, carefree people, who seemed to be living in the moment. I had spent my whole life thinking about the future and how I would fit in and thrive. But everyone around me that night was concerned with nothing more than that party.

With a deep, shaky breath that I hoped no one noticed, I entered Nicole's apartment. I recognized lots of friendly faces from the rush meetings, and plenty of new ones, too—Nicole introduced me to many of them. I hoped that in the weeks to come, I would run into them on the way to classes and say hello, stopping to chat before we went our separate ways.

As the party wore on, an endless stream of people made their way in and out, but I was totally content to stay put and watch. I recognized a bunch of Limp Bizkit songs that I used to hear while huddled alone in my dorm room. But this time, there wasn't a TV dinner in sight.

I followed Nicole, who insisted I call her "Coley," into the kitchen and watched her mix a few red cups with alcohol and juice.

"Hoochies!" she yelled teasingly across the room to a few sisters dancing on the coffee table. Then she turned her attention to me. "All right, what would you like, Peanut? Or should I call you Hollywood because of that cute little car of yours?" she asked.

Surprised and happy that I had a nickname of my own, I paused. I had no idea how to answer her question.

"What do you suggest?"

She studied my face and smiled. I had "newbie" written all over me.

"Well, do you like the taste of alcohol or no?"

I thought back to the time that we helped Papa move out of his house. My uncle Scott and uncle Bobby, both drinkers, were there, too, and one of them had a vodka on the rocks that I had mistaken for a glass of water.

"I definitely do *not* want to taste alcohol," I said with a laugh. "Have anything fruity?"

"Sure do, Peanut!" Coley added a splash of coconut rum to a red plastic cup filled with pineapple and orange juice. It tasted sweet and satisfying. By my second cup, my cheeks felt warm and my lips tingled. We plopped ourselves on the couch and talked, meeting other students as they came through the party.

"You need to come over more," she said. "And get out of your room."

I promised I would.

"There's another party tomorrow night—you're coming." It was an order with a smile. And just like that I had plans: real plans with new friends, sisters, and no need to go home for the weekend. I couldn't stop smiling.

"So what's with the crutches?" Coley asked, her legs curled underneath her and her arm stretched out across the back of the sofa. I sat facing her with my back pressed up against the armrest.

"I had surgery," I answered, taking another sip of my drink.

"What kind of surgery?"

I was stunned by her question. It had always been so obvious to me what surgery I needed. Could it be that from Coley's perspective I didn't look all *that* different? The thought thrilled me, as I told her about what I'd been through.

She was the first person I ever shared my story with besides Mike.

The fall of my junior year, UMass looked completely different to me than when Mom and I pulled up for the first time. Shades of red, yellow, and orange took over the campus, which no longer looked dreary and cold. I framed the photos of Mike and me and put them up all around my room, so that when my girlfriends came over and asked, I could tell them all about my guy from home, just as they talked about their friends from high school.

And when Thursday nights rolled around, the bustle of pre-party preparations no longer scared me. This year, I was right in the middle of it, smiling and laughing in the cloud of hairspray and girlfriends.

As for my dad, he eventually adjusted to the idea of his little girl going off to college. And I adjusted to the difficulties that used to feel insurmountable to me. I even crossed the street in the winter when it was snowy out! I just took my time, greeting friends along the way. I felt like I could do anything.

I seemed to be making friends everywhere I went, too, because at first, whenever there was a significant snowfall on campus, I'd schlep out to my car with a friend or two, prepared to spend a couple of hours digging it out. But each and every time, I'd find my roadster dry and ready to drive off on a side street lined with snow-covered cars. I always figured a maintenance worker on campus knew that it was harder for me to dig out my car than it was for other people and lent me a hand. I even left the worker a thank-you note and a little bag of cookies once for all the help.

One morning, after about a foot of powdery snow had fallen overnight, a sorority sister saw me on the way to class and said she saw a man digging out my car around two a.m. after the snow had stopped. I asked her what he looked like, hoping to hunt him down through the school to thank him. But her description matched someone else I knew, right down to the wool hat and gloves and shuffling gait.

It was my dad.

Every time it snowed, he would drive the hour and a half to campus to dig out my car. He never told me he did it, either. And if my sorority sister hadn't spotted him, I might never have known.

# CHAPTER 13

# My Knight

My marine pen pal in his boot
camp graduation photo.

DESPITE GETTING OFF to a rough start, my college years eventually became the best of my life. I did everything I could to make up for being stuck in the blue recliner during high school and in my dorm room freshman year. I joined the literary society and the UMass Dartmouth Theatre Company, tried my hand as fundraising chair in Phi Sigma Sigma, and took every opportunity to meet new people. My dorm room walls grew cluttered with photos of friends and memories. I dined out often with my sorority sisters, which made the memory of eating processed, gravy-soaked Salisbury steak from the microwave seem laughable. I promised myself that I wouldn't ever take my new friends for granted.

I never wanted to leave UMass, and when the time came to graduate I didn't feel ready to give up the free, fun-filled life I had fought so hard to achieve. Beyond the campus was a bigger world, and I was confused about my place in it. Away from the protective walls of my dorm room and all the familiar faces I had come to love, the real world felt far too big for me to fit into.

The outside world also became more violent and unforgiving than anyone could have imagined. On September 11, 2001, in my junior year, I awoke to a frantic phone call from my mom, urging me to turn on the news.

"We're being attacked!" she shouted over the phone. "I can't believe this, we're under attack!"

I stumbled out of bed and flipped on my TV, and within minutes there were knocks on my door. Everyone in my hall huddled together, speechless as a second plane hit the World Trade Center and the towers fell.

The attacks on our country made me angry and I wished I could do something about it. I wanted so badly to maintain my family's military tradition and enlist just like my Papa and my mom had done. I would have felt so proud—and I know they would have, too—if I had been able to follow in their footsteps. But I would never be physically capable enough to do so.

So it was bittersweet whenever a recruiter would call looking for me.

"Good afternoon! I'm looking for Tiffanie DiDonato," the recruiter for the air force would begin. I wondered if he looked like the recruiter I'd so admired in the living room when I was a little girl in Douglas. "Have you given any thought about what you want to do with your life?"

If he only knew. Respectfully, I declined the offer to go to his branch office, but made sure to thank him for his service.

Before I knew it, young men were missing from my classes, called to duty, and their plans to graduate were put on hold. It was one of the most piercing moments in my life, a time when I truly despised my disability. But since I couldn't serve abroad, I discovered that the act of serving could also mean doing something on the home front.

Like many people all over America, my sorority sisters and I began signing up to write to the troops and attending various care package events in our hometowns. Local malls set up kiosks to send an e-mail to service members and the government joined in with Web sites dedicated to connecting a solider or marine with a voice from back home. It didn't matter if you knew them personally. The need to help, to reach out and connect, was a strong one. Everyone around me just wanted to help and find a way to be involved.

After I graduated and settled back in at my parents' house, I felt the need to continue supporting the troops in a war that was quickly defining my generation. Before long, one of my sorority sisters stumbled upon a military networking Web site and forwarded it to me. At first glance it looked a lot like a dating site. The setup was the same: post a picture, write a little bio, describe your interests, and check the reason you were joining. I was skeptical, but one of the options to check was "pen pal."

"What the hell," I said to myself, staring at the screen. I had done worse on the computer. It was just another outlet to connect to someone far away from home who needed to know that his service meant something to his fellow Americans. Eventually, stories began airing on the news about deployed combat troops who didn't get any mail at all. It broke my heart. I logged into the site, clicked on "pen pal," and posted my bio and a simple head shot. I didn't get many hits, but when someone did write to me, I made sure to respond right away and send off a letter and a care package.

I sent a lot of mail to various soldiers, sailors, and marines. My friends came over and we tied little yellow ribbons around Tootsie Pops and those became care packages in their own right. We put so much thought into each one we sent. For one marine deployed to Iraq, Lance Corporal Arthur Viana, and his platoon, my mom and I canvassed Middlesex County for donations. In the end, we gathered ninety pounds of coffee from various Starbucks, Dunkin' Donuts, and grocery stores. The FedEx employee who helped us with our customs sheet was amazed that two ordinary people who didn't belong to an organization would show up with so much to send, with no particular reason.

"Why are you doing this?" she asked.

"Why not?" I replied.

About a month or two later, I woke up to the sound of our doorbell. A bouquet of gorgeous yellow roses had arrived at my door from the newly promoted Corporal Viana. The card read: *Thanks for making me smile!!! So I hope this makes you smile as well!! Love, Arthur.*

Other troops who received our letters and packages called the house to thank my mom and me. It wasn't a big deal to give out my number. These were America's finest. It felt good to get to speak to them and I'm proud to report that I still casually converse with some of the troops to whom I sent care packages. I'm sure I didn't play a huge part in their safe return, but I did the best I could. I jam-packed every box and at the end of the day, I felt as if I had found my own way to serve my country. I may not be able to dig a trench, shoot a fifty-cal, or fill a sandbag, but damn it, I could give support. I could be a friend.

One cold night in the middle of January 2005, I logged into the site and noticed a message from Lance Corporal Eric A. Gabrielse. Dressed in his blues, his hands in front of him in a modified parade rest, he stood straight and proud in his photo, but there was no hint of a smile. I thought that was a little odd, considering many of the photos of other service members showed at least a touch of happiness, or at least a casual stance. In his message, he explained to me he was stationed in North Carolina, part of the Marine Corps infantry, and he was leaving to go on his second tour of Iraq in July. He told me that he didn't get much mail during his first tour and he noticed in my profile that I was a writer, so he figured it would be nice to have a pen pal. His message was genuine and, like me, he was just looking to connect during the war. I couldn't click "reply" fast enough.

When I wrote back I gave him my instant messaging contact, despite the fact that it was strictly against the rules of the Web site. After a few chat sessions, I gave Eric my phone number. He called two days later and I was struck by how his voice sounded— deeply alone. Our conversations weren't all that spectacular at first. They were very basic. We talked about movies, favorite foods, music, and other random likes and dislikes. I asked where he was from and this led to the discovery that we were natural baseball rivals—Eric's hometown was in New York; mine, outside of Boston. This discovery coaxed him out of his shell and we playfully teased each other about the Yankees' and Red Sox's stats and star players.

Before long, I decided to send him an early draft of my memoir. It was a work in progress, but I wanted him to know who I was. More than that, I wanted him to know who I was not—a five-foot, ten-inch busty blonde with smooth, sexy legs. I knew what it was like to suffer and to force yourself to fight. I knew what it was like to feel exceptional physical and emotional pain. Most important, I knew what it was like to lose someone you care about for reasons you don't understand. I wanted to be up-front and honest. I also wanted him to feel more at ease talking to me. We were fairly close in age and got along well in our casual chats, so I wanted to make sure he knew I could be a real friend and not just a fair-weather one. Maybe he'd been through some shit during the first tour and he could very easily go through a whole lot more. I needed him to know I could relate on some level. I'd been through a lot, too.

If nothing more, should he need it, I could provide an ear to listen, and a shoulder to lean on if he wanted to unload or vent. Worst-case scenario, I thought, he wouldn't read my work, or he'd be too freaked out to carry on any relationship at all. I hoped for the best.

Later, he called me while standing duty at the barracks.

"I read it," he said, his voice deep and booming. It reminded me of Papa's. In the background there was shouting and whistling that brought me back to living in my dorm room. Before I could thank him for reading or ask what his thoughts were, he continued.

"I'm impressed. You could say that I've fought my battles and you've fought yours," he said. "We're both veterans, just different wars."

I was flattered by his analogy. I felt brave and oddly recognized. Honored, almost. With such a simple sentiment, he did more than validate everything I had been through. He appreciated it.

"I know this sounds really weird, but I would like to meet you," he said. His voice turned softer, genuine, and kind. "I've never met anyone with dwarfism before, someone who has gone through bone-lengthening surgery. It would be cool to meet a person who knew what it was like to crawl out of hell but still keep a smile on their face."

I'd been picturing him while we were on the phone, long before he even brought up the idea of meeting. I wondered what it would be like to look into his eyes in person.

"Yeah, it would be cool to meet."

"I don't even know how that would work, but it would be nice. Put a face or something to the letters beyond just a photo, ya know?"

We finished up our conversation in our usual, casual way, but there was nothing casual about what swirled around and around in my head. And maybe even a little in my heart. I sent many things overseas to troops, but I have never met any of them. There was a part of me that thought it sounded a little creepy, but I mulled over the concept that night as I got ready for bed. Washing my face, I suddenly felt a sense of lightness and an urge for adventure at the idea of going to meet my pen pal marine.

Why not?

Nothing was stopping me. Who said I couldn't pick up and go for a weekend? Wasn't this why I'd had surgery—to live life to the fullest? To get up and go when I felt like it, and not let my body stand in the way? I didn't have any expectations. I was just a girl who wanted to show support, and he was a guy in need of it before he headed to war for the second time. If I didn't go and he became another soul sacrificed for our country, I would hate myself.

Early the next morning, I approached Mom over breakfast. She listened as I recounted my conversation with Eric.

"Why not?" she said, just as I had the night before. "But only if I go with you." That afternoon, we researched flights together.

The weekend of January twentieth, we took off for North Carolina. Dad was less than thrilled. Mom and I had always done our own thing throughout my life with all my surgeries and our decisions.

"What should I do if the plane crashes?" he asked.

"Make sure to go to our funeral," my mom quipped.

Though it minimized my sweet father's concern, I couldn't help but laugh.

As I hobbled down the narrow aisle of the plane, Mom stuffed our weekend bag into the overhead storage bin. I stared at her, nervous that I'd made a mistake in rushing to book a flight. The choice to board a plane and meet a perfect stranger who didn't even know I was coming topped my personal list of crazy.

"Mom, I didn't call Eric to tell him we were coming this weekend," I told her. I didn't mean for it to be a surprise, but I'd gotten caught up in the thrill of booking our flight and being spontaneous. And whenever I pictured myself telling Eric that I was coming, I felt like a stalker or an overexcited little girl.

"That was smart," she replied, plopping into her seat and motioning to take my cane. "Call him when we get to the hotel."

"What if he can't meet this weekend? What if he's somewhere out of state?" My worries and worst-case scenarios were having a party in my mind as the captain announced over the speakers that we'd be taking off on time.

"Then you have a nice weekend away with your mother."

Negative thoughts continued to haunt me when we landed and drove our rental car to the Millennium Hotel in Durham. In our suite, with my heart beating fast and my palms sweating, I dialed Eric's number into my cell phone, feeling like I had definitely done something creepy.

When I revealed the surprise, he sounded stunned, but very happy.

"I'll head out to see you around seven tomorrow night," he suggested. "We can hang out, maybe get some pizza?"

"Sounds great!" I responded. I couldn't stop smiling all night.

It wasn't until eleven o'clock on Saturday night that Eric finally walked through the door. Mom had booked our hotel suite near the airport, not realizing that Camp Lejeune was three hours away, in Jacksonville. It took him four hours to reach me because he kept getting lost.

The moment I set eyes on him, I realized he was every bit as striking as in his picture. He had a strong, perfectly square jawline, a cute cleft in his chin, and those long eyelashes that girls always envy. There was, however, one big difference in Eric's appearance in person. He was smiling. The online photos showed a man in uniform—a rough, tough, and disciplined marine just like the ones I remembered from my childhood at the car wash. But that night, he arrived in civilian attire—a blue short-sleeved shirt with tattoos peeking out from underneath, jeans, and sneakers. He had shed his camouflage skin and taken a more approachable form. The only trace of military I could readily spot was his high and tight haircut. His broad shoulders and strong physique made me feel like I was three feet tall again.

I sat on a stool at the breakfast bar in our suite's mini kitchen. As he approached, Eric went from being another service member on a Web site to someone very real. He made Prince Charming look like a pansy. He shook my hand and I was surprised to notice it was soft and smooth—not what I expected at all. I thought for sure his hands would be weathered, worn, and scarred. These were supposed to be hands that could kill a man, but he gripped mine ever so gently.

Eric kept referring to my mom as "ma'am" and offered his hand to her as well. Everything was "Thank you, ma'am," "Yes, ma'am," and, "No, thank you, ma'am." It made me tingle. I'd heard a lot of this in Texas, but I wasn't old enough then to fully appreciate it.

Our conversation in person flowed just as easily as it did over the phone. We smiled, laughed, joked, and hardly realized that the pizza we ordered tasted like particleboard.

Eventually, we made our way to the television in the living room. We ordered *Red Eye* and *The Skeleton Key* on pay-per-view. My mom excused herself to the bedroom. Eric and I had a great time picking apart the plotlines and the acting. I felt comfortable and at ease lingering in our instant connection. After the movies, like two warriors back from fighting, we compared our battle scars.

"Check this one out," Eric said with a grin as he pulled up his jeans to reveal a scar on his knee. "I got this one in high school playing softball."

"Oh, please. I've got you beat," I replied, rolling up my sleeve to flaunt the deeply embedded knots in my forearm.

"That's fucking awesome! All right, now . . ." He rolled up the other leg of his jeans. "What about this one?" He revealed, proudly, a vertical slash across the back of his calf. "This is from concertina wire from my time in Iraq."

I appreciated his effort but was having too much fun playing with him to say so.

"Seriously? You call that a scar?" I mimicked Crocodile Dundee's Australian accent and raised my loose-fitting black pants to reveal my shin. "Now, *this* is a scar!"

"Nice!" he said with a laugh.

In all my life, I had never smiled as much or as naturally as I did in that hotel room. Despite traveling hundreds of miles on a whim, I felt like I was right where I belonged. When my pen pal marine looked at me with his perfect, almond-shaped eyes, I felt something I didn't think was possible in such a short amount of time. But there was no denying it—it overtook me like a wave. I'd never given much thought to love at first sight before, but I was convinced, beyond a shadow of a doubt, that this was it.

Our movie marathon critiquing and snacking took us well into the three a.m. hour. I fell asleep sometime after that, but Eric stayed awake. He didn't sleep all night. Instead he did what a marine is trained to do. He kept watch over me and made sure I never rolled off the couch.

Around six in the morning I woke up but didn't open my eyes. I felt Eric holding my hand, bending my little fingers, and slightly tightening his grip. I wanted to see what was going on, but the last time I opened my eyes only a sliver, I saw my dad crying at the edge of my hospital bed. The last time I had the urge to take a glimpse at the world surrounding me when it thought I was asleep, my heart sank with sadness. That Sunday morning, I allowed myself to peek at the romantic scene unfolding before me.

Eric was smiling softly as he held my hand in his. He was studying it, becoming fond of it, appreciating every detail that made it unique. He gently raised my hand to his lips and placed a tiny kiss on my fingertips.

By the morning, Eric and I both knew what we'd found in each other. But our love story wouldn't be long and drawn out. We didn't have the luxury of taking our time and getting to know each other like other couples. Literally, we had only five months (four, really, factoring in his infantry training in California) before he would be shipped off to the sandbox. We took advantage of every passing day. Though we never discussed it, we both knew that once a marine was over there, God only knew what would come next.

For Valentine's Day, Eric flew up to Massachusetts to see me. He didn't approach his platoon sergeant before purchasing a ticket. He didn't request special liberty before leaving the guarded gates of base or even ask for permission from his squad leader. He just did it, without a single word. We visited Higgins Armory Museum in Worcester, dined out, took dips in the hot tub at my house, and rented nearly every movie available. His visit flew by. It didn't matter what we found ourselves doing, even the most mundane activities were a blast because we were together.

In the weeks that followed, my mom planned a couple more trips to the beaches of North Carolina so I could see Eric. But as the time ticked down closer to his deployment, while I appreciated my mom's efforts, I wanted him all to myself. I wanted to travel on my own.

Before my first solo flight, Mom took me on an impromptu visit to Victoria's Secret. To me, the store had never meant anything more than a place to get cotton panties, flannel pajamas, and robes. The idea of being sexy (or wearing undergarments that looked the part) had never factored into my world before.

"Can I help you ladies with anything?" asked an employee wearing a headset and dressed in a black suit.

"Actually, yes. Her boyfriend is a marine," Mom blurted out as I suppressed the urge to blush.

"Oh. And he's coming back from the war?" She smiled at both of us.

"No, he's going to war," my mom replied. "For the second time."

"Oh, wow, I gotcha," she said. "So you need something to make some memories with?"

I stood there silently, feeling happy with a side of awkward.

"Exactly," my mom continued. "She's going to visit him in North Carolina and they need to make some memories before he deploys."

The lady's smile grew even wider. She started walking through the store and motioned for us to follow.

"Are you sisters?" she asked over her shoulder.

Finally I got a word in. "No. She's my mom."

"Wow. I wish my mom was cool like this."

My mom grinned, clearly flattered. "What can I say? I'm a realist."

I rolled my eyes and followed the clerk as she led the way to a particularly scandalous spot in the store that reminded me of the Pussycat Dolls and Christina Aguilera. It was nothing but hot pink ribbons, ruffles, and binding black corsets accented with rhinestones. This was a frilly satin sex festival and I was about to buy a ticket. I didn't feel awkward about having my mom with me. After all she and I had been through, sex was hardly an embarrassing topic.

But I did feel out of place, as though my life were suddenly on fast-forward. I never considered myself sexy or the type to prance around in suggestive lingerie. I knew many of my friends loved me as a person. I had been someone's friend, close friend, or even best friend, but I was never someone's true love. I might have been adventurous, lively, funny, and loud, but never the object of desire. For someone to be in love with me, and for him to want to express that love, was entirely different. That kind of love meant I would have to be a woman. Up until this point I was catching up on just being a girl.

Meandering through the store, I felt inept, gauche, and nervous. Without much warning, a desire that was tired of being suppressed finally surfaced. All at once, I wanted to look good enough to eat. Even if I feared being eaten alive.

I glanced at a few outfits, while Mom mocked a few others, and eventually I made my choice: black satin boy shorts with a rhinestone butterfly in the back, and an electric pink corset decorated with black ruffles across the bust. I made my way to the dressing room. When I lifted my shirt over my head, wisps of hair fell carelessly out of place from my short ponytail. My mom waited outside the dressing room and made small talk with the lady helping us.

I heard her criticize other garments outside the dressing room. "Why bother wearing anything at all?" Mom quipped about one of them.

"Some of it's ridiculous. Plus, it lasts for only five minutes, then it's on the floor," the lady said, laughing along with her.

I fumbled with the row of black hooks on the hot pink corset. Then I attempted to slide on the boy shorts, but quickly realized bending down in a corset went against the natural order of things. I had to start over, undo the corset, pull up the shorts, and then fumble with the hooks of the corset top all over again.

"Does it fit? Do you need a different size?" the lady asked.

"I'll tell you in a minute," I replied. "I haven't got the damn thing on yet." Convinced that I must be missing the instruction booklet, I took a deep breath. *C'mon, Tiffanie,* I coached myself. *You've taken out your own stitches and staples! For years you cranked your bones apart—you can handle a few hooks.*

Then I pictured Eric, and I became caught up in my reflection in the mirror. I pulled the elastic out of my hair, which fell and shaped my face in a surprisingly flattering way.

I liked what I saw, because I felt confident about the person I was buying this little getup for in the first place. The fit of the boy shorts around my bottom made my legs appear even longer and the corset flattered my hips, hugged my waist, and lifted my breasts. As I examined myself in the mirror, thoughts of Eric running his fingertips from my shoulders to my hands made the knotted scars on my arms virtually disappear. I fantasized about his tight grip around my waist, pulling me so close against him I could feel the warmth of his dog tags against my skin. Visions of him kissing my shins and thighs erased the years of abuse on my legs. Lost in my dream world, I liked what I saw in front of me.

"Are you okay?" the lady asked. I didn't realize I'd been silent for so long.

"I'm definitely okay!" I called out.

Despite the struggle and the ugliness of all the pain I'd experienced, I felt beautiful when I pictured myself with Eric. I felt normal. It was as if all the messiness I'd been through had been airbrushed away, and what remained was my true self.

I was beautiful. And I was ready.

I called out once again beyond the dressing room door. "I'll take it!"

On May 20, 2006, I boarded a plane by myself for the first time. My mom helped me check my suitcase, the sexy lingerie tucked deep inside. I was seated in an airport wheelchair, and an attendant pushed me down the long tunnel to the plane. Walking long distances will always be an uphill battle for me. Settled into my seat, my Steve Madden platform shoes firm and flat on the ground, I left Boston happy, stress free, and enthused—like any other girl jetting off to see her boyfriend. When the flight attendant asked if I wanted a drink, I opted for a screwdriver and enjoyed every sip of it.

For forty-eight hours, Eric and I never left our hotel room. Though I had a rough idea of how the choreography was supposed to go, I let him take control. I put my trust in him and he didn't abuse it. He treated me so delicately, so respectfully, that any anxieties I had drifted away. In his arms, every move he made was magical. Eric's tenderness made me feel innocent again.

As we lay together, I felt appreciated for being both a warrior and a girl he loved. "You know what I can't figure out?" I asked, partially to be cute and partially because I genuinely wanted to know.

"What's that?" he asked while he rubbed my shoulder with his thumb and index finger.

"Where did you put your white horse?" I asked with a wink.

He chuckled a little bit and kissed my forehead and then my hand. "Oh, I traded him a while ago."

I smiled. "You traded him?"

"I traded him for a rifle."

On the thirteenth of July, Eric deployed to Iraq for the second time. He didn't want me to fly down and wait with him as the buses loaded his company.

"It's too hard to say good-bye to you in person," he explained. I thought I heard a crack in his otherwise solid voice. Even though I cried my eyes out, he was right. It was easier to just say "see you later" over the phone. I wouldn't see him again until February.

As I waited for his first letter to arrive, I ordered a T-shirt emblazoned with the words *Half My Heart Is in Iraq*. Immediately when it arrived in the mail, I threw it on. My marine pen pal had become *my* marine.

# CHAPTER 14

# Homecomings

Reuniting with Eric at Camp Lejeune
after his second tour in Iraq.

When Papa's memory started to go, he had to move to an assisted-living facility. Mom said it was because he had forgotten the stove was on and set a glass bowl of linguine on the burners. "Things are getting worse," she said night after night. And she was right. He couldn't recall how to work his VCR or his record player, and the voices of Frank Sinatra and Dean Martin no longer filled his living room.

Every time I had a chance, I climbed into my roadster and took off down Stevens Street, enjoying the tight, winding roads and the wind in my hair on my way to Whitney Place Assisted Living Residences in Northborough to break Papa free and take him to Dunkin' Donuts. Whitney Place was like a mini resort with a kind staff, and also my first employer—I worked at the front desk three days a week and every other weekend. Each time I pulled around the circular driveway, Papa was waiting on a bench, smiling broadly and waving at me, as though I might confuse him with another grandfather sitting outside.

"C'mon in, let's blow this joint," I said one afternoon and waved him into the car. He slowly lowered himself down into the passenger seat and leaned over to kiss me on the cheek. I had the top down and the sky above us was crystal blue and cloudless. Papa adjusted his trusty white Nike golf hat and pulled his blue golf slacks up toward his hips. Within a minute or two down the highway, a cluster of gray clouds formed above us, interrupting the abundant sunshine.

"Looks like rain," Papa said, gazing at the sky intently.

"Don't worry," I replied. "The sun's still out, we'll be fine."

We drove along in comfortable silence, the wind whipping at my windshield as I turned up the volume of my Frank Sinatra CD—which I always made sure to have in the car when I was going to see Papa. I navigated the road toward Dunkin' Donuts.

"Tiffie," he said more insistently, "listen to Papa. I think we better put the top up. It looks like rain any minute."

"Oh, Papa," I said with a smile. "You worry too much. We'll make it to the drive-through and back to Whitney Place before any rain."

We ordered our coffees—a Hazelnut Coolatta for me and a hot black coffee for him—and I turned toward the parking lot exit. Then the sky opened up. Within seconds, we were soaked and I scrambled to find us a parking space through the blinding sheets of rain.

With Sinatra's "Summer Wind" still blaring from the speakers, Papa and I looked at each other and burst out laughing as raindrops continued splashing our faces and rolling down our noses. Papa just shrugged his shoulders and smiled.

"That's life," he said. "That's life."

When our Indian summer ended for good, and fall began to show its true colors, Papa's life grew even cloudier. No longer would he be waiting on the bench outside. He'd be in the common living room area, fast asleep in a chair. Our trips out together ended, and I'd make our Dunkin' Donuts coffee runs alone. Then I'd silently place the drink on the table beside him and sit on a nearby couch until he woke up, or sit behind the front reception desk to work.

I'd answer phones, greet residents and their families, and sort mail and newspapers, and when the night grew quiet, I'd make personal calendars: one for my new exercise routine to help me be free from my cane by the time Eric returned from Iraq, and the other to count the days until February when I would be in his arms again. Like the sight of the clothes I'd ordered from catalogs and the roadster commercial I watched over and over as if it were a big-screen blockbuster, these calendars helped me envision and focus on the day my marine would be home. More than that, they helped me ignore the persistent fears that Eric was dodging rocket-propelled grenades and IEDs—improvised explosive devices—out in the desert.

I found myself daydreaming about what that day would look like when he returned to me. I pictured big band music blaring somewhere in the background as the American Coach buses triumphantly pulled into a parking lot at Camp Lejeune. Crowds of friends and family would be dotted with waving American flags as everyone waited anxiously for the doors of the buses to fold open, revealing our men in uniform, home safe. And then there would be me, standing caneless in perfectly fitting jeans, kitten heels, and my soft velvet jacket with a satin bow. My makeup would be perfect and my hair adorably curled, and I'd top off the look with the crystal heart necklace Eric bought me, plus a coat of vanilla lip gloss—his favorite. And when I finally saw my marine in his digital desert uniform, I'd jump into his arms with one knee bent like they do in the movies and he'd dip me into a long, passionate kiss. The scene looked a lot like the ones from the 1950s films I had loved to watch with Papa growing up that were now collecting dust on his bookshelf.

That winter, my morning trips down the curvy driveway to the mailbox grew slower. The cold always wreaked havoc on my joints, and the ice and snow building up on the driveway made the walk even more perilous. But I never stopped making those trips, with my cane in one hand and a pink envelope sealed with a heart sticker in the other. I wrote every day and every night, and sometimes two or three times in one day. I did everything to keep Eric updated on all that was going on, even if the only change had been in my appetite—he knew about it all.

"Have you heard from him, Tiffie?" Papa would ask at Whitney Place, propping his elbows up on the counter of the reception desk. Though Papa struggled to remember so many things, he never forgot to ask about Eric.

"I have!"

I looked up at Papa smiling, pushing aside my worry. "Want me to read you the last letter he sent me? I'll get it for you, Papa."

"Sure," he replied, "let me get another cup of coffee first."

"I'll make it for you, Papa."

By six p.m., the phone fell quiet at the front desk. Papa had settled onto a couch in the communal living room. I made my way to the coffee machine, making a full black cup for him and a half-cup with cream and sugar for me. I walked carefully, without my cane, trying to push my progress a little bit more each day.

Carrying our coffees and my letter to the couches, I walked

past the baby grand piano that was almost never played. Then I opened Eric's letter and began to read.

*I love you, baby,* the letter began. Papa sipped his coffee and sat back on the couch with a soft smile and a faraway look in his eyes.

*So I wake up today to the sound of HMMWVs and a seven-ton, which meant resupply was here. Sure enough I was right and I found two letters and a postcard waiting for me. I helped move water and whatever else they needed done and then went to your letters. Let me tell you it's been a hard week, so getting your letters really lifted my spirits. I've had a toothache for the past 8 days. Mix that in with missions, patrolling, the heat, lack of sleep, a lot of physical work and stress—it's been a bad week. But I'm feeling good because of your letters. God, I love you.*

As I continued reading aloud, I noticed a few residents making their way down the main hall. There was Trudy, a real riot who moved quickly despite her wooden cane, and Connie, the no-nonsense lady who loved nothing more than a spirited debate. They both joined us in the living room to listen to my letter. Then Marion, a prim and proper uptown gal, came in with Mr. Rochette, a marine who served in World War II. Before long, I had my own listening party—about a dozen residents who all gathered in the living room around me and Papa each time I received mail from Eric. They all listened intently, and I noticed the occasional smile or twinkle in their eye when I'd read phrases like *I can't wait to come home* and *I love you.*

When I finished the most recent letter one frigid afternoon, Papa pulled out a piece of paper from his pocket. It was a picture of a dog making snow angels. Beside it, he had written: *An officer on duty,* a good-natured dig at the men in charge of my enlisted boyfriend.

"Give this to him in your next letter. It'll make him laugh."

I showed my audience, who'd gathered, as always, in the pastel chairs. They laughed, and then Papa and Mr. Rochette began playfully chiding one another about their respective military ranks.

Soon, it wasn't just Papa asking how Eric was doing, but also Mr. Rochette, Marion, and Connie, too.

"I got one!" I'd tell Mr. Rochette as he passed by the desk on his way to dinner, showing off my latest letter.

"You did? I'll let everyone know."

At six p.m., I'd leave the phones again and join the group in the living room to read. We'd all help ourselves to a cup of coffee first, and then meet by the piano. One night, Trudy took the longest to join us, so I waited for her to begin. When she finally came around the corner, urging me to begin in her usual peppy tone, I noticed she was carrying a framed photo with her.

"Go ahead, Tiffie," she urged again, settling into her spot by the fireplace. "Go ahead."

*I got a phone account, baby*, I began, stealing a glance at Trudy, who had propped up the photo next to her. *I'll finally be able to call you over here.*

The group murmured with happiness at the news.

*I told my buddy about all the letters you write me. He said, "Wow, she must really love you." And I replied, "Yes. She really does."*

When I finished the letter Trudy was the last to return to her room. She slowly followed me to the reception desk and revealed what was in the frame: her wedding photo.

With tears in her eyes and her hands shaking slightly she said, "He was an airman." She touched the glass softly. "He would have loved to hear your letters."

I stared at his pale face and wavy blond hair, thinking how alike he and Eric might have been. Despite the generations between us, the residents and I bonded each night in the living room, supporting one another and listening to one another's stories about loved ones either overseas or long gone. They became my closest friends.

After I read Eric's letters, our conversations often turned to the war going on in the Middle East and how much we'd all like to help. That Christmas, we figured out a way to do just that. Since the troops couldn't be home for the holidays, we would ship the holidays to them, in individual stockings stuffed with goodies. We called it Operation Stocking Stuffer.

We set a date that winter to have an event at Whitney Place to stuff the stockings and ship them to Iraq. I reached out to local schools and asked if teachers would help their students to make holiday cards for the men and women in Eric's unit. I called popular rock radio stations and asked if they'd mention the event to help bring in donations. The response was overwhelming. Teachers jumped at the chance to help, and not only were the radio stations helpful, but they also sent us supplies of their own: CDs, band merchandise, gift certificates, DVDs, and books. Soon our little idea had grown so big that the closet that Whitney Place had lent me to store our supplies was overflowing and I had to take on a second, then a third, then an entire room to store supplies. People from around town came to Whitney Place with beef jerky, crackers, and cookies to send. Local coffee shops and even the big chains delivered coffee by the pound. The love and support was monumental.

So was the cost to ship all this stuff to Iraq. I needed help. Luckily, all it took was one phone call to the Marine Corps League in Worcester—the people there promised to ensure every package was sent by setting up fund-raisers of their own.

Finally, on a cold, blustery afternoon, the main event for Operation Stocking Stuffer had arrived. The crowd came in droves. The Junior Marines attended, and community members funneled through the Whitney Place doors. There were teachers, students, family members of residents—everyone came and they brought piles of stockings and supplies with them. In the bustling sea of people, I made out a woman with long blond hair tied in pigtails underneath her baseball cap. My mouth dropped open and I felt my eyes water when I finally placed her. It was Mike's sister, Maureen.

"I heard about the event on the radio," she said with a smile when she saw me.

I hugged her tightly, sobs escaping me.

"Don't cry," she said. "He would be so proud of you and he'd want to be here. I'm proud of you, too. And I brought friends," she added with a wink.

A group of people next to her grinned broadly, each one holding stockings, snacks, and handwritten notes.

"Where do you want us?" Maureen asked.

I led her and the rest of the team past a reporter and cameraman from the local news station, a line of people picking through items for their stockings, and Edna Sinclair, a resident who was sneaking a pack of cigarettes and a five-dollar bill into her stocking. Another resident, a man named Ed, had squeezed into his half-century-old sailor uniform just for the occasion. Papa was there, too, standing with my mom and smiling, observing everything and everyone as he always loved to do. That Christmas would be the last time I saw him that way.

On February 6, 2007, on Camp Lejeune in Jacksonville, North Carolina, Eric and the rest of 3rd Battalion, 2nd Marine Division, Lima Company were scheduled to arrive at seven p.m.

The clock on my mom's dashboard read 6:40 and we were still trying to find a parking spot in the massive lot on Camp Lejeune. The scene looked nothing like I had pictured.

It was a million times better.

There were big white tents with tables full of food and drinks underneath them. A DJ got the already excited crowd even more pumped with patriotism. Moms, dads, wives, girlfriends, and children all danced and jumped up and down, anxiously awaiting the big arrival. I was trying to find a spot among them all. Then the DJ interrupted the music.

"Everyone! I just received word that the buses have pulled through the gates of Camp Lejeune!" she shouted into the microphone. The crowd roared. Mom looked panicked.

"The camera!" she shouted. "I can't find the camera! I think I left it in the car!" She bolted back to grab it.

I stood by myself—in my perfect outfit and without crutches or a cane, just as I'd pictured—in the middle of the huge, happy surge of people. The white, unmarked buses with black-tinted windows rolled through the gates and into the parking lot. I had no way of knowing which bus was Eric's. The crowd erupted in cheers. I craned my neck and tried to see through the masses, asking Mom, "Do you see him?" over and over again. Everyone was either crying as they found their loved ones or still holding handmade signs high in the air so their marine could spot them. I walked through the throngs, unsure of which direction to go. Maybe I should just stand still and let Eric find me, I thought to myself, when his friend Martin spotted me first.

"Hey!" Martin shouted. "Tiffanie!" He hugged me and thanked me for the Christmas stocking. "Turn around," he said. "Turn around real quick."

And there he was. Before I could say a word, Eric hoisted me high in the air and then lowered me down to his chest. My tears soaked his camouflage shoulders as I kissed him. Several minutes later, he gently placed me back on the ground and my mom called to us.

"I got it!" she shouted, waving the camera triumphantly. "I got the picture!"

That night, we settled into the rental beach house that Mom and I had found for Eric's homecoming. It was nothing fancy, but it had a big deck overlooking the ocean. The three of us ate dinner and Eric filled in my mom about all he'd done overseas. Then he and I sat on the deck and listened to the waves crash, marveling at being back together again. As I held Eric's hand and breathed in the salty air, I felt as content as I'd ever been. We'd planned to rent an apartment together in North Carolina just outside of base when he returned. Eric was contemplating reenlisting into the Marine Corps and that meant I would need to find a new job away from Whitney Place—away from the residents I had bonded with over the past seven months.

"Marry me," Eric said out of nowhere. "Marry me tomorrow."

I sat up to face him. Marriage seemed a little ways off yet. There was so much we still had to figure out.

"What?"

"I want you to marry me tomorrow. After we sign the papers for our apartment, I want to marry you."

"But what about the whole tradition thing?" I asked. "What about asking Dad for permission and all that? What about a ring?"

"I'll do all that, too. Just marry me."

"I can't," I told him. "It doesn't feel right." It's not that I didn't want to spend my life with him, though. I felt safe with Eric and, more important, I felt I could be myself with him. I could expose my scars, both internal and external, and he appreciated each one of them. I could feel that love every time he looked at me. I didn't have a single question about him or about us. He was undoubtedly the one for me, but I couldn't see myself saying "I do" without the presence of the one man who believed in me from the day I was born—Papa.

After Eric's homecoming in North Carolina, I went back to Massachusetts to spend time with my family for a few days before moving in with Eric down south. One night back at my parents' house, Mom tiptoed into my bedroom around four a.m. She squeezed through the boxes I'd packed and sat on my bed and put a hand on my shoulder, waking me. Sleepily, I inched upright to face her. Her cheeks were stained with tears.

"Papa's gone."

* —◆— *

My uncles joked that it was just like Papa to see that a blizzard hit just in time for his funeral. It made us feel better to think that he was there and making things difficult, creating a huge winter storm so everyone wouldn't feel so sad.

Of course, we cried anyway. Eric and I made our way into the cemetery in my uncle Joe's Lincoln Town Car. Eric was decked out in his dress blues, his white-gloved hand resting on my thigh as we drove. I slipped my hand in his and squeezed as we pulled into the cemetery. Everything was white, and in the distance a half dozen sailors stood around an open plot with their rifles pointed upward. Eric helped me out of the car, asked if I was okay to walk through the snow on my own, and excused himself to speak to one of the sailors standing by Papa's coffin.

I shuffled through the snow, shielding my eyes from the elements, and caught up with my mom and Aunt Jean. Everyone huddled close together and I watched as Eric stood at attention next to the brass handles of the casket. People were sobbing all around me. My uncles wrapped their arms around my mom as the pastor read aloud.

Soon, it was time to fold the flag that was draped over Papa's casket. I watched as the sailors worked in unison, hand over hand, to fold the flag into a crisp, perfect rectangle. Then one sailor turned and presented the flag to Eric, who, stiffly at attention, presented the flag to my mom, raising his arm to salute her. Through tears, she smiled at Eric and thanked him. Mom would later tell us that she had to fight the urge to leap forward and hug him.

I stood in front of Papa's grave silently when it was all over, once everyone had gone back to their cars. I wanted to tell him I'd never forget the movies we watched and the lessons he taught me. And I wanted to assure him that I'd always keep fighting. But no words came out. Eric stood at my side and rubbed my shoulders. Then he put a hand on the casket.

"I'll take care of her now. I promise."

In the car on the way home, I wondered about my grandfather on my dad's side. Pauline had died from cancer years earlier. He was the only grandparent I had left.

After Papa died, I quit my job at Whitney Place. I couldn't bring myself to return. I knew I would struggle too much with the memory of him in the living room where we'd gathered to read my letters. I was ready to leave, start anew, and begin my life with Eric in our tiny apartment in Hubert, North Carolina. I had come a long way. It seemed like centuries ago that I couldn't reach light switches, faucets, or even my own ears.

Life was waiting for me.

One week after Papa died, Eric and I were preparing to head from Marlborough to North Carolina in our rented U-Haul. While I got ready at my parents' house for a dinner date with Eric, he

was secretly looking for my dad. Dad, however, was doing his best
to outrun him in a fruitless effort to stall me from growing up. I
think my father knew Eric's intentions, but he wasn't ready to face
them. So he kept moving in the hope that Eric would give up and
that I would stay a little girl for a little while longer.

Mom knew it, too, as she followed, giddy, behind Eric in his
pursuit.

"Jesus Christ." Mom sighed, out of patience with my dad's
avoidance. "Gerry!" she shouted. "Would you stop walking for
one goddamn minute?"

Dad was officially cornered in the spare bedroom. Mom
watched over Eric's shoulder as he pulled a black velvet ring box
from his pocket.

"Sir," Eric began softly, "I'd like to ask you for your permission
to marry your daughter."

"Oh . . . you are serious," Dad responded, as if my moving in
with Eric hadn't tipped him off about where our relationship was
going.

"Yes, sir. I am."

Dad paused, then smiled and shook Eric's hand.

An hour later at the restaurant, I sat next to Eric on the arm
of one of the couches in the waiting area at the Olive Garden. I
mentally sorted through our U-Haul, wondering if we had everything we needed and whether the overflow would fit Eric's Ford
Escape.

The blue recliner was not coming with us.

My clothes, jewelry, and bedroom set were all carefully packed
into the truck, along with a dozen Home Depot cardboard boxes,
red plastic bins, and a set of unmatched luggage. We would buy
our living room and dining set in North Carolina and I looked
forward to perusing the aisles of the furniture stores together.

The hostess called us and we were seated, but Eric quickly excused himself to the men's room.

I waited in the booth, growing antsy when he didn't return for five minutes, then ten. I wondered if he was sick in the bathroom. Would this affect our drive to North Carolina in the morning? The waitress had come and gone asking for our drink order, but Eric still was nowhere in sight.

When the waitress returned to my table she asked that I get up and move. "We actually have a better table for you both in the back," she said. "Would you mind moving?"

Confused and slightly annoyed, I agreed.

"Will you let him know where I am?" I asked, gesturing to Eric's empty seat. "He went to the men's room."

"Sure," she replied, motioning for me to follow her. She led me around a few tables and through the private dining room.

"Right through here," she said, but then she stopped and stood off to the side. I stood next to her, anticipating another waiter rushing by with a tray full of food. But no one came.

It took a moment to fully process the scene: the balloons, then the familiar faces of my aunts and uncles and my friends from college. Even Johnny, Eric's best friend from the marines, was there. Finally, I noticed Eric standing in his dress uniform beside my father in the corner. I stared at him, trying to make sense of the scene with a hopeful inkling about what was about to happen.

Slowly, Eric walked toward me with a giant smile and dropped down to his knee. I hardly thought this would happen for me now. I always felt so behind the curve. Friends of mine in college who didn't even have boyfriends at the time had all the details of their proposals planned out. They spent hours daydreaming about the particulars of the ring they wanted, the perfect "will you marry me?" speech, the perfect guy. Some had even picked out names for their future children.

I never had. But now it was happening.

"I love you," Eric said. His face was red as he blushed in response to all the eyes on him. "Will you marry me?" He opened the box to reveal a sparkling diamond heart set in white gold. My very own heart-shaped ring.

I could hardly choke out a word and excitedly nodded yes.

The waitresses were clapping, and crying, and in the corner, gripping my dad, Mom did the same. In what seemed like an instant, my family had gone from pain and grief to smiles and tears of happiness.

That's life.

My engagement story unfolded just as I would have written it myself—sweet, spectacular, and surrounded by the people I love. Even Papa was present in his own way. As Eric slipped the ring over my finger, a new song came on over the speaker system in the restaurant.

Frank Sinatra's "Summer Wind."

# CHAPTER 15

# Admired

Our wedding day.

AFTER A BUSY year of planning my wedding and coordinating the arrival of Eric's groomsmen from Iraq, the big day was just around the corner. I was having fun with all the preparations, but thoughts of my grandparents began creeping into my planning and nagging me even in my dreams. The idea of not having a single grandparent watch me get married made me sad.

Eric and I were back up north for the weekend so I could attend my bridal shower. Leaving Eric in bed to keep sleeping, I slipped out of the covers, pulled on my robe, and headed downstairs to walk through what had become our wedding staging area.

In an array that stretched from the dining room, through the kitchen, and into the great room stood sixteen tall, potted trees that would line the aisle at my wedding ceremony. In the kitchen,

Mom joined me for a cup of coffee. She'd been staying up late at night for months, wiring crystals to every branch of the trees.

"Why pay someone to do it when I can make it look just as nice?" she'd always tell me.

I wanted an enchanted forest theme for my wedding, complete with peacock feathers, deep red roses, and tons of sparkle. In his usual fashion, without consulting anyone, Dad had trucked through the woods and came back with bare trees to decorate and make into my decor. I wanted a forest and he brought me a forest.

I lifted the filter out of the coffee machine, emptied it into the trash, then turned the faucet on and rinsed my hands. I still took so much pleasure in these tiny independent motions. Even as I was enjoying preparing coffee for Mom and me, the dream about my grandparents continued to haunt me. But there was nothing I could do. Three of my grandparents had passed away and I hadn't even seen my paternal grandfather, Jeremiah, since I was a baby.

After breakfast, I began getting ready for my bridal shower, hoping that the dream—and my feelings of sadness and regret—would fade. I didn't want anything to take away from my special day. My shower was held at Maxwell-Silverman's in Worcester. It had a retro jazz club feel. There were toy hot air balloons decorating the ceiling, adding a feeling of whimsy. Everyone who was important to me was there, from sorority sisters to friends and family. Even the nurses who helped take care of me at my worst came out to celebrate. Now they were seeing me at my best. They were all excited to sip mimosas, indulge in multiple desserts, and play shower games.

But I couldn't stop thinking about how a wedding is supposed to bring together not just a bride and groom, but our families as well. And mine was only half represented. I'd discussed this with my mom, but why hadn't I done anything about it? I thought I was brave, strong, and ready for anything life threw at me, yet I could barely gather the courage to ask my dad about his relatives. Was I really that tough if I didn't do anything about it?

In an instant, my good feelings about the guests at my shower melted away. Sure, I loved everyone in the room, but who *wasn't* there? Then, like another gift placed in front of me to open, I got the answers to my questions.

From behind my table, an army of women I'd never met before filed into the room. It was Dad's side of the family. Mom had invited them but wanted it to be a surprise.

One by one, holding gifts of their own, they introduced themselves.

I remained quiet and listened to all their names, shocked and wondering if it was all real. Mom stood up to hug them.

"Thank you for coming," she said.

"Thank you for connecting with us after so long," one replied. "We wouldn't miss this." She turned to me and introduced herself as my aunt Marsha.

I had an aunt Marsha.

"Hello, nice to meet you," I said, my voice and hands trembling. I had aunts, cousins, and second cousins standing before me, all with loving smiles. And they would be there for my wedding.

A few days later, I woke up and followed the same path through the potted trees to the coffeemaker. I emptied the filter, filled it with fresh grounds, and waited to fill my mug. But as Mom and I settled into our chairs, I gathered the courage I wasn't sure I had.

"I'm going to call him," I told her. Then I looked up my grandfather Jeremiah's number, picked up the phone, and dialed quickly before I could change my mind.

It rang for only a moment and then I heard the voice of a cheerful man on the other end.

"Hellooo?" his voice sang out.

"Hello . . ." I paused, unsure of where to go from there. "This is Tiffanie. Your granddaughter."

The seconds that followed felt like an eternity. My heart raced.

"Yes!" he shouted into the phone. "Hello, hello, hello! How are you?"

I felt my face flush as I heard how happy he sounded to be on the phone with me.

"I'm very well," I said, fidgeting. Mom stood at the other end of the kitchen counter, fighting back tears. "I heard you are coming to my wedding and I want you to know that I'm so happy," I continued. "I . . . I would love to see you before then." I flung the idea out there like a rock loaded into a slingshot, unsure of where it would land. But at least I tried.

"Yes!" he said excitedly. "Now. You come now!"

"Right *now*?" I wasn't prepared for his response.

"Now. I'll be here waiting."

"What did he say?" Mom asked, practically jumping up and down. "Tell me, what did he say?"

"He said he wants to see me *now*."

Her eyes sparkled. "Then let's go!"

We dashed around the house and threw on some clothes. I hurriedly applied makeup and spritzed myself with my favorite perfume. Then I called the one person I talked to about everything.

"He said he wants to see me now!" I told Eric, who'd returned to Camp Lejeune. My voice was shaking, my mind racing. How had I gone this long without speaking to or hearing from my grandfather when all it took was one damn phone call for us to plan our reunion? "What do I say when I see him for the first time? What do I do?" I asked Eric, nearly panicking.

His answer was beautiful in its simplicity.

"Baby, you say hi, just like you did over the phone."

In the car, Mom called Dad to tell him where we were going. "Good," he replied simply. Dad's reaction stumped me. If he felt it was so natural that I was going to see Jeremiah, why hadn't he initiated it years ago?

I decided that my father really just hadn't known how to do that.

"Tell Papa I said hello," Dad said.

Papa? The name was so familiar. I repeated the word over and over until it started to feel real. I had *another* papa.

Jeremiah's two-story home was decked out with autumn decorations. A gold and red wreath with plastic pumpkins greeted visitors at the front door, along with a festive fall flag waving in the wind. His cute barn-shaped mailbox marked the house number and we parked beside a tall, white privacy fence. I heard voices and laughter from the backyard and the fence was open, like a sign that I was welcome to walk in.

So I did.

Mom led the way and I followed quietly behind her, not sure what to expect. I didn't even know what Jeremiah looked like. What would he think of me? Did I look like a DiDonato, or more like the Pryors of my mom's side?

From behind the small backyard swimming pool, my new papa stood up the moment he saw me and made his way toward us. We met right in the middle of the yard.

His arms were outstretched and so I extended my own and we embraced. It was automatic, like nothing at all, as if I had only returned from a long vacation. There were no words exchanged.

I didn't have to say anything and neither did he—the tears that trickled down his cheek said it all.

Though I had lost one grandfather, I had somehow found another.

• ◆ •

The floor of the hotel suite felt solid beneath the balls of my feet, a sensation that never got old. From inside my satiny stockings, I dug my toes into the rug and squeezed. The scene around me was like a dream: all of my best girlfriends chatting and laughing, their matching Swarovski crystal peacock broaches glittering on their red dresses.

Today was my wedding day.

The October air in New Hampshire was cool and crisp as it breezed through the open window—a welcome change from the warm suite buzzing with activity. Across the room, Mom unzipped my wedding gown on its hanger and noticed me watching her. *I love you*, she mouthed and I smiled back.

She had a look on her face that I'd never seen before, one that went beyond just the pride that a mother feels for her daughter on her wedding day. It was as if Mom, too, had dreamed of a moment like this every day that I went through the bone lengthening.

And now here it was.

I had chosen a white satin Anne Barge gown with a crisp, delicate bow sewn inches above the empire waist. In it, I looked so delicate, like I had never endured a single ounce of pain in my life. I loved feeling that way for once.

"Close your eyes," my makeup artist, Mija, said softly. I settled into the plush hotel room chair as she gently swept shadow across my eyelids. We'd discussed the look I wanted—a vintage fairy-tale feel—and I was sure that she'd deliver. Mija was beautiful herself and had her own vintage flair, right down to the feathers she'd pinned in her hair.

"How are you feeling?" she asked while dabbing glue along my lash lines to secure a pair of dramatic false eyelashes.

"I'm nervous," I replied in a whisper. I felt jumpy and antsy, too, but I wasn't sure why. Eric and I were already technically married. Six months earlier, we'd eloped, officially saying our vows in front of a justice of the peace in a basement room at the Onslow County Courthouse for twenty dollars. Our decision made the most sense, given my insurance needs with my move out of state. But I knew I wanted to spend my life with Eric and getting married right away with a big wedding to follow seemed like the best of both worlds. No one knew but my mom and, thankfully, she understood. She had always been spontaneous. Her only disappointment was that she wouldn't be there to share in it with me. Afterward, Eric and I met with our chaplain on Camp Lejeune and he assured us that what we had done was very common among military couples. It was also very understandable, given all the sacrifices involved in military life and love.

But the nerves were still there as I anticipated walking down the aisle. Everything I'd gone through with my surgeries felt cut-and-dried, definitive. I *had* to get through them to achieve my goal, and despite all the risks, I somehow felt in control. Even if that was an illusion, I had my battle plan, and that was that. I just wanted to be proud of myself. Getting married, with two families involved to boot, felt far more complicated.

Now I wanted to make sure everyone else was proud of me.

"Everyone I know is going to be downstairs taking their seats," I told Mija. "I want them all to be proud of not just me, but Eric, too. I want everyone to be proud and happy for us, together."

"They will," she assured me. "This is your day. You've done enough fighting. Just relax today. Breathe. And have fun."

Maureen Gould put her hand on my shoulder and winked. I was honored to have her as part of my wedding party.

"Close again," Mija told me and I obliged, taking a few peaceful moments to reflect as the glue on my lashes dried. As Mija worked, I loosened up and laughed along with my girlfriends as they recounted the funny stories from my bachelorette party a few days earlier.

With overflowing champagne glasses, my friends and I had partied all the way to Jacque's Cabaret in Boston. Nine of my sorority sisters and my "Gay of Honor," Mark, whom I'd met in college theater, had planned to celebrate with the fabulous drag queens at the cabaret. The whole night was hysterical. As my friends—wearing coordinated T-shirts decorated with inside jokes about me and Eric—laughed and drank all around me, my fears about walking down the aisle surfaced.

"What's wrong, love?" a performer called Diamond asked me before taking the stage.

"I'm getting married soon, and I'll be in front of *all* my friends and family," I blurted out—my last martini giving me the courage to open up to a total (but terribly fabulous) stranger.

"I don't know how to walk down the aisle without my cane and I wish I did. I'm afraid I'll trip or forget how to walk."

She grabbed my hand and pulled me toward the stage with her. "Honey, that aisle is *your stage*," she said and my friends applauded and screamed at the sight of me up there with the performers.

"Always be confident about who you are," she said, shaking her sequined dress at the crowd. "Throw your head up high and *own it!*" With a dramatic snap of her fingers, she summoned the DJ to turn on her music and she stomped across the stage in her stilettos.

"Let's go, sister," she said, urging me toward her. "Your turn! Come *claim* your man at the end of that aisle!" Laughing as I mimicked Diamond's confidence, I threw my head back and followed her across the stage, with the whole bar cheering me on.

"Claim your man!" my sorority sister Nicole repeated in our hotel suite, cracking up the group. That night, I'd dropped my cane defiantly, tossing aside my fear and uncertainty as I marched across that stage.

So what was stopping me from marching down the aisle, too?

In the back of our ceremony ballroom, I stood clutching my bouquet of garnet-colored roses and white stephanotis sprinkled with glitter, crystals, and feathers. I felt like the Wedding Day Barbie I coveted as a little girl. But Barbie had nothing on me.

Standing at the beginning of the aisle, I took in the scene: deep jewel tones decorated the room, and the aisle was lined with the trees my father had chopped down, glistening with crystals. I held my bouquet in one hand just beneath my stomach, as I had been shown, and gripped my dad's hand in the other, partially for balance so I could make it down the aisle without my cane. But I would have held his hand even if I didn't need it—I was so happy he was by my side and that I was able to show him, in the most extravagant way, that my days of lying in bed in pain were over.

A custom runner ran the length of the aisle and read *Eric & Tiffanie: Always and Forever.* It was almost too pretty to walk across. I stepped gingerly toward our chaplain.

During the rehearsal dinner, he told me to walk very slowly down the aisle. I felt relieved to hear that. But seeing so many familiar, smiling faces, I felt such a rush of energy that I almost wanted to run. I was ready to become Mrs. Tiffanie Gabrielse and I couldn't wait to be embraced in front of everyone. I wanted the whole room to know I was happy.

With each step I took, Eric's smile seemed to grow wider until it took over his entire face. I felt my heart racing and I took a deep breath to calm myself down. Someone had advised me to really take in the moment at my wedding, because it goes by so fast. With every lift and swing of my legs, and with each squeeze I gave my dad's hand, I tried so hard to notice everything around me and commit it all to memory.

I saw Dr. Mortimer, along with pretty much every nurse that had ever taken care of me. I smiled at my friends and my cousins and uncles. Our eight groomsmen, all in their dress blues, waited at parade rest by the altar and our eight bridesmaids, all holding deep purple calla lilies, smiled at me.

As we approached the chaplain, Eric walked slowly toward me, and Dad placed my hand in his. Then he gave me a little kiss on my forehead. If he had to face giving his little girl away, I knew he was happy that he was handing me over to Eric. I smiled at him, and then at our guests.

Eric's hand felt soft in mine, like the first time I had ever touched it in that hotel suite in North Carolina. His palms weren't sweaty and there was not a single quiver as he held my tiny hand tightly in his. The music floated to a close and the chaplain opened with bits and pieces of the letters Eric and I had written to each other during his deployment.

As he spoke, I peeked again at everyone in their chairs. My Papa Jeremiah was there, in the front row in a suit and tie and red rose boutonniere, smiling.

After our short ceremony concluded, I felt incredibly proud to walk back down the aisle with Eric as husband and wife.

A flurry of photos later, the air was charged with excitement as we entered through the double doors to our reception ballroom. The band announced us and our eight groomsmen moved forward from the head table. As we approached, Johnny bellowed out into the ballroom.

"Draw swords!" he ordered, bringing his sword high in the air, matching its tip with that of the one directly across from him.

Hand in hand, Eric and I passed underneath and our initials in lights floated across the floor. Keeping with Marine Corps tradition, Johnny dropped his sword in front of me and didn't allow my passage until Eric and I kissed one more time for all to see.

"Welcome to the family!" Johnny shouted over the clapping as he tapped me on the behind with his sword.

I smiled and gave a good wiggle, flaunting the bustle of my gown.

"Withdraw swords!" Johnny ordered, ending the drill and commanding the marines to take their seats.

I had gained so much in such a short period of time: all my new relatives, Eric's family, and now, the Marine Corps. The wedding, or as Eric and I called it, "Our Show," was playing out right in front of us, and he bent down to kiss me for what felt like the hundredth time.

As the night wore on, I made sure to go around and thank each of our two hundred guests. Seeing everyone together and so happy felt like a photo album unfolding before me. In one shot my dad and my mom were smiling, dancing, and happily greeting our friends who'd traveled to be there. It was as if all of the fights that had flared up between them during my childhood were nothing more than distant memories. In another snapshot, my Papa Jeremiah was clapping, standing, and smiling in my direction, urging me to keep dancing. And then in another, Errol and I shared a smile. I made my way over to him and asked him to dance.

There wasn't a single moment that I was able to sit down. Nor was there a moment that I wanted to. Inside my platform sneakers with the ribbon laces that I had picked out for dancing, my feet throbbed and ached and felt like they might burst.

But I didn't care. I danced for hours. I held one corner of my dress just as I had seen other brides do on TV and jumped into the cliché conga line that eventually formed and traveled around the room. I felt like a kid again, twirling around as my dad's stereo filled the room with music.

And when the band began to play "You Are So Beautiful" and Dad met me in the center of the ballroom to dance, he took my hand and whispered, "I'm proud of you, pumpkin pie. You've always been so beautiful to me." As we danced, he repeated the chorus each time in my ear. For that moment at least, my dad was extremely, undeniably happy, and that was a picture I'd never forget.

At two a.m., the lights in the ballroom kicked on. The band and the DJ had both played their last song. I sat at one of the round tables with Nicole and a few other sorority sisters. My uncle Bob, carrying my little cousin Cassandra passed out in his arms, gave me a kiss and headed out the door while Mom and Dad thanked the videographer and photographers. Eric came up beside me and furrowed his brow a bit when he noticed me wince. Then I let out a little chuckle that grew into full-fledged laughter.

"You okay, babe?"

"My feet hurt so bad I could die," I said, still laughing. My reaction took my friends by surprise.

"If you're in pain why are you laughing?" Nicole asked.

"My feet hurt," I responded.

"And how is that funny?"

"Because," I began, "if my feet hurt it means I got to use them!"

I continued to laugh. It was the most welcome pain I'd ever felt. I felt that I could do anything, and I'd found more for myself than I ever thought I would. It was a feeling that dwarfed everything else I'd been through.

•—◆—•

Nearly skidding down the stairs from my bedroom, I clung to the banister for dear life. Stairs will always be my nemesis. But on the Monday morning after my wedding I was not about to let them win. I looked into the kitchen and noticed my dad already up preparing coffee. I let out a shout from the belly of our home and aimed it upstairs.

"Hurry up! It's almost on!" I yelled to Eric and my mom, who were still making their way down. The local press surrounding me and Operation Stocking Stuffer had attracted national press. *Good Morning America* put together a piece about my surgeries, concluding with a few photos from my wedding day. During a teaser before a commercial break, there I was, a "medical marvel," with a photo of me next to the old Pontiac on our kitchen TV screen.

I was really on television.

"Let's go, let's go, let's go!" I called out again. And down the staircase they came, my dad handing coffee mugs to sleepy family members as they entered the kitchen. We all piled into the theater room, the one room in our house that didn't have a window. I think Dad wanted to watch it play across the big screen like a real movie.

Side by side we sat, motionless and speechless as the five-minute segment aired on national television. In that small time frame, *Good Morning America* captured my life, my struggle, and in the end, my fairy tale. At the end of the segment, viewers were invited to discuss the piece on the ABC online bulletin board, and we all clamored off the couch and over to the computer to see what people would say.

Minute by minute, people offered their opinions on my story. I was surprised, but still intrigued. The majority were very supportive and one even called me and Eric "America's Sweethearts." Several people were amazed at the courage it took to drop everything and relentlessly focus on a goal.

One woman wrote that she could relate to what I'd been through, having been teased terribly through her childhood. She said she was horrified that Ms. Hart had gotten away with treating me the way she did and she congratulated me on the way I chose to live my life.

If only it remained strictly positive.

By nine o'clock that morning, the controversy began. Perfect strangers spoke out against my decision to have surgery and criticized me at will. I never realized how strongly the world would react to my desire for independence.

By ten, I received an update from a producer that my story was one of the most read on the Web site.

But it was only just beginning. The feedback from sharing my story followed me all the way back to North Carolina. And it went far beyond just the ABC site. I was inundated with messages on my Myspace account and my personal e-mail. People thought I was shallow and vain for undergoing my surgeries and said that I shouldn't mess with what life dealt me.

I made the mistake of programming my cell phone to notify me each time I received a new e-mail and for the weeks that followed my press, my phone alerts were relentless. "You have a message. You have a message. *You have a message!*" my phone sounded constantly.

After reading the final e-mail in my in-box one day, I shut my laptop and made my way into the living room, where I plopped down on the couch next to Eric. He flipped through the channels on our TV and I threw my legs over his on the coffee table. We were watching *our* TV, I thought to myself with a smile. And in *our* living room! I picked up a pile of mail off the arm of the couch, dropped it on my lap, and began to thumb through it. Some envelopes contained our bills, and I was eager to hold them in my hand. It felt as if they were some kind of validation that we officially shared a life together. Others pieces of mail were advertisements, the same kinds of ads that my mom would toss aside and proclaim to be junk. I loved junk.

And then, slipped into the middle of the pile, was a single letter that I was not expecting. There was no return address.

Dear Tiffanie,

As a little person myself, I feel that I need to share my opinion with you. I can't believe you advocate this procedure when it is reckless, dangerous and careless. There was no mention of the numerous complications that can occur because of this procedure and yet you flaunt it as though it is a cure for dwarfism. Who are you to suggest dwarfism is wrong or that it needs to be cured? By undergoing surgery that is what you are doing. You are advocating this belief and you should be ashamed. You are a disgrace to the dwarf community.

I was baffled. I never said anything about a "cure," for dwarfism, nor did I suggest that it was wrong. And suddenly, I was a sellout, a disgrace to the little people community and its culture?

I wanted to flick a light switch without using a spatula.

I wanted to reach the faucet without first reaching for a stool. I wanted to see over the counter, take out the trash, and make my own coffee without something or someone assisting me. I wanted more for myself, more out of life, so I changed my body to that end. I'd never given any thought to what the "dwarf community" might think about that. But here I was being judged, as if I'd gone against some sacred order of Dwarfdom.

I stared at the letter for a while, mulling over the words and debating if I should try, somehow, to respond.

"Babe?" Eric said. "Babe, what is it?" He eyed the letter in my hand.

I handed it to him with a smirk and watched his eyes scan across the page. He tightened his lips together and instantly I saw it bothered him more than it bothered me.

"It's like my Papa always said," I told Eric before he had a chance to speak. "Opinions are like assholes. Everybody's got one."

I wondered what would have happened if I had subscribed to this belief in high school. Would Ms. Hart have affected me in the same way? Would I still have had the surgery?

The answer was a resounding yes. The world would never adapt to me, so I adapted to it. Having surgery was about living the life I'd always dreamed of. And here I was, actually living it! I smiled at Eric, thinking, *knowing*, that I never would have met him if it weren't for the transformation I'd undergone.

"This really doesn't bother you?" Eric asked. His expression had softened, and I could tell he felt proud that I wouldn't let some stranger's ignorance get me down.

"Nope—I have much more important things to do than worry about that," I told him as I eagerly snatched the letter out of his hand. I walked from the couch to the garbage can in the kitchen, dropped the letter inside, and turned back to Eric with a smile.

"Like taking out the trash."

# Epilogue

*W*HETHER YOU LIKE *it or not, you are and always will be a dwarf. The sooner you accept it the better. What if your child is also a dwarf? What are you going to do, make him or her go through the procedure as well? God help them. You will be an appalling parent.*

Of all the unsolicited advice and opinions I got after my *Good Morning America* segment, this one stuck with me the most. It underscored the fact that the decisions I may make for my child one day could be far more difficult than those the average parent faces. If I have a baby who is born with diastrophic dysplasia, would I encourage him or her to go through with the surgeries that I did?

I'd have to think about the answer to that question sooner than I expected.

As of the writing of my manuscript, I am seven months pregnant! Eric and I have always wanted to have children but the timing wasn't exactly planned.

"You said from the beginning you wanted to live life," Eric said when we got the surprising news. "Well, babe, that's exactly what we're doing! We're starting our family."

The news of my pregnancy also turned out to be an unexpected lesson in genetics. In my early doctor's appointments to determine whether our baby might have diastrophic dysplasia, Eric and I were both tested to see if we are carriers of the single gene that causes my unique condition. While I am a carrier of the gene, we found out that Eric is not, so there is only a very slim chance that our son (we're having a boy!) will be born with diastrophic dysplasia. Of course, there's always the potential that he could be born with a different form of dwarfism. The truth is, I am more likely to have a baby with dwarfism than an average-size mother.

I don't have any expectations for parenthood. As of right now, I'm just having fun picking out names, shopping for baby clothes, and seeking out the perfect crib. I'm excited and looking forward to the little things, like watching Saturday morning cartoons with our boy. I can't wait to watch Eric read to him before bed, and for family trips to military appreciation festivals and dressing up our little guy for Halloween.

I'm also scared out of my mind. For starters, I don't know how I'll give birth. This is a brand-new ballgame for me that doesn't involve an osteotomy or anything to do with bone breaking or pins—I'm totally out of my element. I have yet to learn what my options are for epidurals or anesthesia when I give birth, because I have a curvature to my spine and I'm a complicated intubation. So far, doctors have told me that a C-section will be the best and safest way to deliver. I've been working on accepting this reality, but I'm so scared to have a doctor take a scalpel across my belly. I know this is a very common procedure, but to me it's new and terrifying to the point that I find myself actually wishing for the days of pins and wires being drilled and strung through my bones. While incredibly painful, those ordeals felt so much simpler than giving birth—and parenthood.

On the plus side, I haven't experienced any morning sickness, aches, or pains. Maybe a higher power figured I've been through enough and I'm finally getting a break.

I do know that at some point I'll have to be put on bed rest because of my size. There has been so much involved with finding the right ob-gyn for me as I'm a high-risk mom and I could have a high-risk baby, too. The whole process has made me feel like I'm fifteen again, trying to find the right doctor who's willing to work with me and perhaps to think outside the box. Except this time, it's not all about me. Thankfully, Dr. Mortimer has joined me in the hunt for the right team of specialists and I've returned to Massachusetts to deliver my baby back home.

Returning to my parents' house up north presented another nerve-wracking situation: having my father see me pregnant. Even the word "pregnant" feels awkward to me (I only refer to myself as "preggos"). On my first day back home, my heart felt like it as going to beat out of my chest as I sat at the kitchen table, waiting for my dad to make his way up the cellar stairs. When he came into the kitchen, I was ready to jump out of my seat.

"Hey, Dad!" I practically shouted.

"Hey, Tiff."

"Don't I look good?" I blurted out, eager to avoid any awkward silences.

"Yah, yah, you look good," he replied, leaning in for his usual light embrace and pat on the hand. My dad has never been one to give out big, warm bear hugs. Then we were stuck in the silence I was trying to avoid . . . until Mom came into the room.

"*Well?* What do you think?" she asked, nudging him on the shoulder. "This is your first grandchild!"

Dad nodded, smiling slightly, but remained silent. I watched fear and worry wash over his face as it did so many times when I was stuck in our blue recliner. I'd need to prove to him all over again that I could be not only independent, but also ready to build a family on my own.

As for Eric, he couldn't be happier. The first thing he bought for the baby was a rattle that says: *The Few, the Proud, the Cute. USMC Baby!* Seeing his gigantic smile as he shakes the rattle near my belly, I think that there's no way I'm not off to a wonderful start.

Of course, I've also been thinking about what we'll do if our baby has any form of dwarfism. To me, it wouldn't be a terrible thing, but I would certainly prefer that he doesn't so he won't have to deal with the pain and worry that I did. I've also had to think about whether I'd want our son to undergo the bone-lengthening surgery that I had as a child.

My answer is an unequivocal yes.

If our son has arms so short that he is unable to reach his own ear, I want to do what my mother did for me and have him go through the procedure for those critical couple of inches. Beyond that, additional surgery would be up to him. If he dreams of washing his hands without a stool, or struggles to boil a simple pot of water, I will support him in doing whatever it takes to live an independent life, even if he faces opposition from others along the way.

Eric doesn't feel as strongly as I do about that point. It's something that we'll continue to discuss and debate over until we are actually holding our son.

But we do agree on this: whether our little boy has challenges like I did, or grows to be six feet tall, I will teach him to be a fighter, to be brave, and to take no prisoners in life. Most of all, I'll make sure my child knows that he should never let anything stand in the way of becoming the person he wants to be.